THE OBEDIENCE PARADOX

THE OBEDIENCE PARADOX

FINDING TRUE FREEDOM IN MARRIAGE

MARY STANFORD

Our Sunday Visitor
Huntington, Indiana

Nihil Obstat
Msgr. Michael Heintz, Ph.D.
Censor Librorum

Imprimatur
✠ Kevin C. Rhoades
Bishop of Fort Wayne-South Bend
July 27, 2022

The *Nihil Obstat* and *Imprimatur* are official declarations that a book is free from doctrinal or moral error. It is not implied that those who have granted the *Nihil Obstat* and *Imprimatur* agree with the contents, opinions, or statements expressed.

Except where noted, the Scripture citations used in this work are taken from the *Revised Standard Version of the Bible — Second Catholic Edition*, copyright © 1965, 1966, 2006 National Council of the Churches of Christ in the United States of America. Used by permission. All rights reserved.

English translation of the *Catechism of the Catholic Church* for use in the United States of America copyright © 1994, United States Catholic Conference, Inc. — Libreria Editrice Vaticana. English translation of the *Catechism of the Catholic Church: Modifications from the Editio Typica* copyright © 1997, United States Catholic Conference, Inc. — Libreria Editrice Vaticana.

Every reasonable effort has been made to determine copyright holders of excerpted materials and to secure permissions as needed. If any copyrighted materials have been inadvertently used in this work without proper credit being given in one form or another, please notify Our Sunday Visitor in writing so that future printings of this work may be corrected accordingly.

Our Sunday Visitor Publishing Division
Our Sunday Visitor, Inc., 200 Noll Plaza, Huntington, IN 46750; www.osv.com; 1-800-348-2440

ISBN: 978-1-68192-695-7 (Inventory No. T2571)
1. RELIGION—Christian Living—Love & Marriage.
2. RELIGION—Christianity—Catholic.
3. RELIGION—Christian Living —Family & Relationships.

eISBN: 978-1-68192-696-4
LCCN: 2022941023

Cover and interior design: Lindsey Riesen
Cover art: Adobe Stock

Printed in the United States of America

For Trey

CONTENTS

CHAPTER 1

THE BIBLICAL IDEAL OF OBEDIENCE

"Let it be to me according to your word" (Lk 1:38). In this single utterance, Mary of Nazareth expressed the essence of what it means to be a person. To our modern mind-set, this may seem an odd claim; in a culture where notions of belief, obedience, and submission are pitted squarely against concepts of knowledge, freedom, and self-assertion, the Virgin's words here might even seem to give us evidence of something weak, ignorant, or slavish that undermines rather than manifests her personal dignity. Why would Mary's consenting reply to the Angel Gabriel, words suggesting a disposition of obedience, represent the ultimate truth about the human person?

An adequate response to this question requires at least a cursory examination of our culture's vocabulary. Today, for example, we tend to contrast belief with knowledge; it is not uncommon to hear "Do you believe it to be true?" or "Do you know it to be true?" in a conversation. Many of us dismiss belief as simply something we are content to settle for whenever we have reached the limits of our intellectual capacity. Others might even classify belief as a kind of lazy or grasping substitute for so-called actual knowledge.

Yet we clearly use the word *know* in different ways. We say we can know how an engine works through observation and experimentation. But then we apply that selfsame word, *know*, to our friend, and it seems to acquire a different meaning. We say things like "I know my friend" or "I know my husband loves me" with ease and certainty, despite a lack of similar empirical verification. Within this broad range of use, however, scientific, empirical knowing appears to be held in higher esteem. The now ubiquitous statement "That's your truth; this is my truth" does not hold up very well in physics class. Scientific understanding of the physical universe seems to be a privileged place, one where so many of us today confine our understanding of what we can know to be true.

What is particularly illuminating, moreover, is the method by which we attain this knowledge. The father of the scientific method, Francis Bacon, summed it up when he wrote that "the secrets of nature betray themselves more readily when tormented by art than when left to their own course."[1] In short, if we are to gain knowledge of a thing, we do it by force; we step back, put on gloves, lay it on a table, and slice it up. But can we apply a similar method to getting to know a person? Can one person ever come to know another through distance and detachment — by sheer observation, experimentation, or interrogation? Try as we may, there is no test, no resume, no social media profile that can prove *empirically* that we really know someone. (It is not surprising, however, that many in our culture try to do this very thing all the time. Whether through the algorithms of Match.com or the billion-dollar industry of artificial reproductive technology, people are fooled each day into thinking they will know just whom they will get when they purchase information or genetic material from sellers who have checked boxes listing physical accomplishments, GPAs, and other personality traits.)

Such attempts notwithstanding, although we might *know about* a person through detached study, we will never *know* a person that way. True personal knowledge never comes through detachment — neither a remote gathering of facts nor a forceful interrogation — but only through a free attachment: the concrete, living encounter known as *relationship*. Personal knowledge, the knowing of persons, is not accompanied by a guarantee — by the kind of certainty achieved through purely material experimentation. But that fact does not make such knowledge any less real. Joseph Cardinal Ratzinger, now Pope Emeritus Benedict XVI, explained:

> I can actively and methodically investigate material things. I can subject them to my control because they are inferior to me. But … another person is beyond my understanding if I treat him in this way. On the contrary, I only come to know something of him when I begin to put myself in his place, to get inside him, by some kind of sympathy.[2]

Because persons transcend the merely material — because they possess an "inside," a spiritual dimension unfathomable by the scientific method — we can only be known through opening up to another person in a kind of union. Moreover, such unions between persons always require trust. Human society would not exist without a grand network of trusting relationships: between spouses, between parents and children, among friends and neighbors, among communities and nations. A disposition of trust is the opposite of the attitude of control we witness in the conquests of Bacon's scientific method. It requires risk — a real vulnerability to the free initiatives of another — and it always includes the possibility of being deceived. It is no coincidence that, following the moral distinctions offered by Aristotle and St. Thomas Aquinas, Dante Alighieri chose to situate the treacherous and the fraudulent — that is, those who have violated special bonds of trust — in the deepest circle of hell in his *Inferno*. Such sins wound human persons so deeply because they tear at the very fabric of community in which we flourish. Personal relationships are essential; therefore, so is an attitude of trust in a fully human life.

A synonym for the free decision — the willing act — of trusting another is *belief*. In the most authentic sense, belief is not a crutch that compensates for some weakness. Rather, it is a necessary disposition for a person, a being who is more than material. The spiritual powers of a person both require and enable us to make a free choice to believe, to trust in another person — whether God or man — in order to be fulfilled. Ratzinger wrote that "belief in the sense intended by the Creed is not an incomplete kind of knowledge, an opinion that subsequently can or should be converted into practical knowledge."[3] As a matter of fact, he explained, "belief has always had something of an adventurous break or leap about it, because in every age it represents the risky enterprise of accepting *what plainly cannot be seen* as the truly real and fundamental."[4] So we are not to understand belief to be a kind of counterfeit knowledge. It is not the opposite of knowing! It is, in truth, the only path to personal knowledge, the only way of coming into full contact with another reality that possesses a spiritual dimension.

The opening words of the Book of Wisdom echo the truth that belief is a prerequisite for knowing a person — even, and perhaps especially, a divine person: "Seek Him with sincerity of heart; / because he is found by those who do not put him to the test, / and manifests himself to those who do not distrust him" (Wis 1:1–2). God is a loving communion of Persons — pure spirit — Who can only be known through belief. Ratzinger explained,

> God is not just something we could ever force to call out at given moments, "Oh, here I am." God is found precisely when we do not subject him to the criteria of falsification used by modern experiments and existential proof. … I can only begin to seek God by setting aside this attitude of domination. In its place I have to develop an attitude of availability, of opening myself, of searching. I must be ready to wait in all humility — and allow him to show himself in the manner He chooses, not as I would like Him to do it.[5]

Without such an act of trust, without a willingness to be vulnerable to the initiatives of another, the possibility of our knowing any person — God included — is hopeless.

The Catholic Church upholds Mary as the "perfect embodiment"[6] of this attitude of availability. In Luke's Gospel, we read that Elizabeth called Mary "blessed" and praised her as "she who *believed* that there would be a fulfillment of what was spoken to her from the Lord" (Lk 1:45). Mary's words of acceptance to Gabriel expressed her leap of faith — a profound movement of trust — by which she willingly placed herself and her future in the hands of an Other, One for Whom it is proclaimed that "nothing will be impossible" (Lk 1:37). Such is the essence of belief: It is first and foremost our response to an encounter with another person, with a *spiritual* being.

Not surprisingly, the concept of obedience is intimately linked to this dynamic. The word *obedience* comes from the Latin *obaudire*, meaning "to hear or listen to." Our Lord himself referred to His mother when He said, "Blessed rather are those who hear the word of God and keep it!" (Lk 11:28). Mary heard. She listened to "what was spoken" and then in perfect freedom accepted what was offered to her.

The concept of freedom is a critical component of obedience. Modern culture tends to oppose the two ideas — as though the more we obey, the less free we find ourselves. One possible source of confusion here is that we often apply the word *obey* to subhuman creatures, such as "a bird obeys his instinct" or "the planets obey the laws of nature." Those divinely created things, however, cannot be said to obey any more than they can be said to disobey. Operating according to instinct or the laws of physics implies that the activities of such beings are necessitated by their very design. We should never think of blaming an animal for its behavior — however unpleasant — because the fact is that we cannot assign an animal responsibility or true agency. It simply experiences an inner force which directs it to its fulfillment.[7] A personal being, however, does not experience such a compulsion from within; a mentally and emotionally *healthy* person's activity is not determined by our nature but is in fact self-determined, or chosen — for good or for ill. (I emphasize *healthy* here because those who struggle with compulsive behavior due to addictions, post-traumatic stress disorders, or similar challenges suffer because they do not experience the full freedom for which they were created, and as a result they are not living a healthy human life. In fact, to experience any recovery or relief from such conditions requires therapies that rely on learning to use our own free choices as humans to create new habits that help free us over time from behaviors once experienced as debilitating.)

Authentic obedience is always chosen, not compelled or forced. As a matter of fact, Aquinas teaches that the opposite of *voluntas* (the will) is *violentia* (force or violence).[8] A true act of obedience is willed; anything less — anything forced — is robbed of its meaning. A slave is one who is treated as less than a person — as one who is forced to serve. To describe slaves as "obedient" simply because they carry out their master's orders under threat of violence is to make a mockery of the term *obedience*. Real obedience is a choice to trust — a free movement of one will to embrace the will of another. Only someone with an ability to understand and with the possibility of choice can truly be said to obey. Only a person can truly consider the words of another and respond freely. Only a person can make the choice to trust someone, to believe in another person, even when one cannot empirically verify the truth of what that other person offers.

A biblical example that illustrates the relationship between freedom and obedience is the story of Zechariah. Upon receiving the message of the angel Gabriel that his aged wife, Elizabeth, would bear a son, Zechariah was incredulous; the angel said, "You did not believe my words" (Lk 1:20). Gabriel perceived that Zechariah was unwilling to trust in God and in His power to bring about such an unlikely event. In the face of Zechariah's attitude, however, God responded in an intriguing way. Zechariah was not punished for his unbelief — not summarily stricken down or forced to undergo some humiliation. Rather, he was purposefully stricken dumb. Unable to speak, he was invited to engage in speech's only alternative: listening. Zechariah spent the entirety of Elizabeth's pregnancy with John the Baptist in silence, the perfect condition for one to contemplate God — to really hear God — without his own words getting in the way. Sometimes our own words reveal only our own preconceived, limited notions of reality. Instead, Zechariah was afforded the opportunity to observe in silent wonder the ways of the divine. Deprived of the power of speech for a time and allowed to really hear and thus to contemplate, Zechariah found that he was finally capable of making a leap beyond himself — a leap of true belief, expressed so joyfully in his own canticle: "Blessed be the Lord God of Israel, for He has visited and redeemed His people" (Lk 1:68).

Mary of Nazareth had no need for the instructive silence temporarily imposed upon Zechariah. Mary was able to respond immediately to God's call in faithful obedience because Mary was already disposed to contemplation. Revered in Catholic tradition for having "kept all these things, pondering them in her heart" (Lk 2:19), Mary has been described by Church Fathers as a contemplative soul who was "in prayer" at the moment Gabriel found her.[9] Nearly every masterwork of art depicting the Annunciation echoes this view, portraying her in a reflective pose, invariably with the Sacred Scriptures close at hand. Mary was ready to respond in faith because she already knew God. Already caught up in humble contemplation of His works, she was not tripped up by any preconceived notions that might have limited God's power. Mary's *fiat* — her "Let it be to me according to your word" (Lk 1:38) — showed her to be someone who heard, contemplated, and freely embraced God as a personal being, not a mere thing, and therefore as One Who can only be known through belief. Mary's obedient service as the "handmaid of the Lord" was not compelled in any way; it was chosen. To suggest that Mary's obedience was slavish robs her of that very gift that makes her a person: her freedom. The modern mind-set that pits knowledge against belief, or freedom against obedience, condemns those very aspects of personal being that distinguish us from the rest of creation: those capacities which echo the truth that God "created man in his own image" (Gn 1:27).

The Church proclaims that when a person believes and makes an act of faith, that person "completely submits his intellect and his will to God" (CCC 143). This word *submit*, which today we caricature as a kind of blind, mindless servitude to another, is really the only way for us to break out of the confines of our own limitedness, of our own selves. Only by employing our capacity to wonder and contemplate, only by making the great and terrible leap of trusting another, can we go beyond ourselves to experience spiritual union. Try as we might, our attempts to live up to modern notions like "self-assertion" and relate to others through domination and control will never satisfy us, because such are the methods of material science alone. When we approach other people in such a way, we reduce them to mere objects and rob ourselves, as well as them, of the possibility of spiritual contact.

Mary did not hold God at arm's length. She did not interrogate Him or "put Him to the test" (as Wisdom said) to guarantee her preservation. Instead, she did something that no lower creature could ever do: She made an act of faith. In entrusting herself to another, as our biblical ideal of obedience, she achieves real spiritual union. In fact, her bond with the Holy Spirit in the moment of the Annunciation is so complete — with no doubts or hesitations held in reserve — it allowed her to bear the very fullness of fruit. God himself took flesh in her womb.

CHAPTER 2

THE STRUGGLE
WITH OBEDIENCE

Belief, faith, trust, obedience. It is nearly impossible to consider any one of these concepts without invoking each of the others. Saint Paul does so precisely when he preaches about how he was sent to bring about an "obedience of faith" (Rom 1:5). For what is faith but an act of trusting belief in another? Scripture declares that "by faith Abraham obeyed" (Heb 11:8) when God called him to set out for the Promised Land, and perhaps even more so when he showed his willingness to sacrifice his beloved son Isaac. The Roman Canon exalts Abraham as "our father in faith." Yet in the *Catechism of the Catholic Church*, the Church declares that although Sacred Scripture gives us Abraham as the model of the obedience of faith, it is the Virgin Mary who achieves "its most perfect embodiment" (144). The Church "venerates in Mary the purest realization of faith" (CCC 149) because she submitted freely to the angel's tidings.

But despite our admiration for these biblical models of faithful obedience, Catholics today tend to fall in lockstep with modern culture in our antipathy toward the term *obedience* in everyday married life. Any mention of a wife "obeying" or "submitting to" her husband is usually met with a chuckle or a raised eyebrow. We might dismiss such terms as old-fashioned residue from a patriarchal past — or worse, they call to mind brainwashing cults that consider women to be property. Many a seemingly embarrassed priest has in his homily skirted the words of Ephesians 5:22: "Wives, be subject to your husbands, as to the Lord." What we often fail to recognize — even amid our modern discomfort with such references — is that our aversion to the notion of obedience is not a radically modern development. It surfaced at the very origin of humanity's relationship with our Creator.

In the opening chapters of Genesis, the serpent tempted the woman with the idea that God was not to be trusted, and that His command regarding the fruit of the mysterious Tree of Knowledge of Good and Evil was not for her and Adam's good, for their protection and flourishing. Rather it was a power play, the serpent suggested: a jealous Creator's attempt to control and manipulate them. Recall the serpent's response to Eve after she protested that she and the man would die if they partook of the fruit: "But the serpent said to the woman, 'You will not die. For God knows that when you eat of it your eyes will be opened, and you will be like God, knowing good and evil'" (Gn 3:4–5).

From the beginning, we see that humanity has been tempted to doubt the very identity of God. Is He a personal God, who can only be known through a trusting relationship? Or is He a mere object, whose mystery is no more than a puzzle for us to solve and appropriate through detached, calculated grasping? If God is an object, then a free creature cannot respond to such a mystery through trust, but instead only through a bold taking of what was not really offered. Viewed in such a light, God's supposed generosity can be dismissed simply as a restriction on our freedom, rather than its source.

John Paul II argued in his Theology of the Body — reflections articulated over the course of his weekly papal audiences from 1979 until 1984 — that no biblical evidence supports such an understanding of God. We have no indication that the Creator is an object to be controlled or a puzzle to be solved. Rather the Bible indicates that God can be trusted. In the first books of Genesis, the primary way in which God reveals himself is as Creator and Giver of everything that exists. When we observe that He was totally free (not compelled) to make or not make the universe, we face the personal reality of God as we reflect on the words, "God saw everything that He had made, and behold, it was very good" (Gn 1:31). Through these words, John Paul II said, "we are led to glimpse in love the divine motive for creation," for "only love, in fact, gives rise to the good and is well pleased with the good."[1] God reveals His power through His love and His acts of giving. The first man and woman received everything, including themselves, from the loving hand of God. From the beginning, they experienced nothing else but God's total generosity and care for them in the Garden. He was the Giver, and they were the grateful receivers.

Yet here, perhaps, is the sticking point: Being the receiver of a gift requires trust. One who receives is vulnerable to the initiatives of the giver. The receiver is invited to trust that the giver offers the gift freely, with only the hope of a grateful reception in return. (We explore this further in chapter 3.) For when someone gives with "strings attached" — that is, intending to use the receiver or to rob the receiver of freedom — the giver makes a mockery of a true gift.[2] The serpent's suggestion, however insupportable, was that God was doing just that. "By casting doubt in his heart on the deepest meaning of the gift, that is, on love as the specific motive of creation,"[3] John Paul II said, man and woman accepted the devil's implication that God is not loving, but jealous — that His command is not part of His gift to humanity but is only a tool to withhold knowledge from us in an attempt to diminish our freedom.

Such a doubting disposition stands at the foundation of the fateful error that we continue to witness today. Our first parents — refusing to make the trusting leap that is essential to knowing a person — mistook God for an object. They were deceived into thinking they could gain "God's knowledge" by force, by "stealing" His secrets, as it were. Sound familiar? Recall from chapter 1 that Francis Bacon, one of the fathers of modern science, boasted of "tormenting" nature to give up her secrets. His words should only highlight our first parents' mistake. Adam and Eve saw that "the tree was to be desired to make one wise" (Gn 3:6) and thought that it would give them power. "Knowledge is power" is the battle cry of modern science; it exalts putting its subjects "to the test" to gain from them useful knowledge of the material world. Such an approach to a person, however, is a fruitless endeavor, for "God's knowledge" is hardly the same as "knowing God."

God is not some object we can study and re-create in a lab. God is a loving communion of Persons! Becoming like God is not as simple as extracting what He knows and using it to imitate Him. That Adam and Eve thought God's knowledge is something separate from God himself reveals their profound underestimation of His identity. God is not a material thing, but a spiritual being. Adam and Eve should have been striving for a deeper personal knowledge of God. But such knowledge comes at a steep price: We can attain it only through a trusting relationship. Instead, Adam and Eve tried to acquire a kind of scientific knowledge of God's secrets. They were duped into thinking that they could become like God by information — some set of facts — rather than by transformation, through a loving and grateful union with their Creator in Whose image they were made. In approaching God as an object rather than on a personal level, they strove to attain knowledge without relationship, power without vulnerability. They allowed the serpent to distract them from the fundamental truth that God's power is manifested first not in His knowledge but in His love — the grand display of His free gift of creation. By seizing the fruit of the Tree of Knowledge against God's will, Adam and Eve were transformed right in front of us, from receivers into takers. They operated outside the dynamic of trust that alone brings about intimacy between persons. Instead, they grasped at what they desired without any regard for the relationship that the initial gift of creation had established between themselves and God.

What Adam and Eve failed to predict was the effect that such an alienation from God would have upon their relationship with one another — an effect that continues to mark our relationships today, and especially our marital relationships. The sudden and rather jarring experience of bodily shame drove the man and woman to conceal themselves from one another immediately after their act of disobedience. This shame reveals a profound connection between personal intimacy and vision. For when we are in a relationship, when we know a friend spiritually, we see differently. Our friendships with others cannot help but affect the way we see the world, as each friend's unique perspective broadens our own. We begin to see as the other person sees and to appreciate things we never noticed before.

John Paul II explained that, prior to the first sin, we "participated in the divine vision of the world," which was "transmitted … by the Creator."[4] Our first parents, by virtue of their intimacy — their spiritual union — with God, were able to perceive reality more fully than they could have with their own powers. The breadth and depth of their divinely enhanced vision is summed up in how the two stood before one another prior to the Fall: "naked, and … not ashamed" (Gn 2:25). In that moment, Adam and Eve perceived the fullness of one another's identities. Each appreciated the entire value of the other and participated in the divine perception of the goodness of creation. John Paul II suggested that their vision at that moment did not "contain an inner break … between what is spiritual and what is sensible."[5] In other words, Eve did not simply see Adam's body — she saw Adam. Likewise, Adam did not distinguish between Eve's body and Eve herself. The sight of her body communicated to him her interior depths, her spiritual dimension — the very foundation of what made her a person. The clarity and consequent joy of such perceptions of one another were the direct result of their friendship with God. They were able to see with His eyes and to perceive one another as "very good" (Gn 1:31). With such perfect vision, they could recognize in one another a truly fit companion with capacities belonging to no mere animal.

Such a perfect glimpse of the truth about one another did not last long. At the moment of our first parents' refusal to receive creation as a gift — to maintain their trust that God is a lover and not a tyrant — we lost our ability to perceive the world as it truly is. Severing themselves from divine intimacy through their own choice, the first man and woman lost their "right to participate"[6] in the divine vision of the world. As a result, all humanity has been consigned to view the world in a limited and partial way. Striving for power and refusing the trust required to be receivers, Adam and Eve effectively refused to receive even their very being as given from the hand of God. As they refused to receive themselves, then, they instinctively lost that full possession and understanding of themselves that they had initially experienced.[7] They suddenly failed to understand who they were. A wedge of fear was driven between them as they hid their bodies from one another with leaves.

Adam's telling response to God — "I was afraid, because I was naked; and I hid myself" (Gn 3:10) — reveals the utter confusion in which man and woman found themselves when they severed themselves from God's enlightening friendship.

Only moments after experiencing the deep, personal intimacy signified by nakedness without shame, the first man and woman were overcome with shame — and they were ready to blame others for their transgression. The woman blamed the serpent, and the man pointed the finger at the woman. Though the couple was unwilling to accept responsibility for their own choice, God nonetheless addressed them with that choice's inevitable consequences. Because they were unwilling to receive the world as a loving gift from God, the world would now elude humanity's peaceful possession and rule. It would resist us with its "thorns and thistles," demanding our toil and pain in our dual mission to "fill the earth and subdue it" (Gn 1:28). Struggling to possess the earth means struggling to possess our own earthly dimension: our bodies, whose desires have proved difficult for us to master ever since.

But consider another consequence of the Fall that we must understand as part of this book's discussion of the paradox of obedience. Man and woman, though "fit" for one another and equally personal beings, are nonetheless not replicas of one another. The consequences of Adam and Eve's refusal to trust God, therefore, play out in a mysteriously asymmetrical fashion. The woman is told that "your desire shall be for your husband and he shall rule over you" (Gn 3:16). These words usher in the reality of what the first man and woman wrought through their disobedience: an impoverishing of love. The man — who once rejoiced that the woman was "bone of my bones and flesh of my flesh" (Gn 2:23), meaning an equal in humanity who is worthy of his love — became inclined to rule over her as though she were something lesser. Her body itself, once indistinguishable from the whole of her person, became subject to objectification and now risks being treated as no more than what John Paul II called / a "terrain of appropriation."[8] By approaching God as an object rather than on a personal level, man and woman now tend to treat each other in the same fashion — taking only what they desire rather than receiving what the other one freely offers.

But again, such a disposition toward the other does not show itself in identical ways. This new human state is marked by a kind of desperate longing on the woman's part, and by desire for domination and use on the man's. The woman seems particularly at risk; in struggling to master her own needy desire for the man, in the sad course of history she has often struggled to see herself as more than an object, even as she resists being treated as an object by men. "He shall rule over you" has become a self-fulfilling prophecy. Eve feared God was seeking only to control her, yet separated from Him, she found that Adam became only too willing to do so.

Since that fateful beginning, the history of the sexes has been marked by what Edith Stein (the twentieth-century German-Jewish philosopher and Carmelite nun, now canonized as Saint Teresa Benedicta of the Cross) called "a brutal relationship of master and slave."[9] Much like the earth, which at that moment began to resist human efforts to till it, woman emerged before man as an obstacle he must conquer rather than as a person to be cherished. At her most vulnerable, woman has been the victim of man's sensual appetite, used and so often abused at his whim; at her worst, she has purposefully aroused man's desires to achieve her own ends, effectively objectifying herself to achieve material or emotional gratification.

Regardless of whether the woman has related to man as innocent victim or calculating seductress, the man too has experienced a reduction of his own personal nature. In attempting to avoid vulnerability while seeking control, man after the Fall has found himself losing control. As he has descended into lust, he has lost that very freedom which set him apart from the animals and has effectively been transformed into what Teresa Benedicta called a "slave of the slave who must satisfy him."[10] The fallen version of the relationship between the sexes makes intimacy — spiritual communion — nearly impossible for the sexes to achieve. Such a union is only possible in an atmosphere of trust rather than fear, of vulnerability rather than control, and of receiving rather than taking.

CHAPTER 3

OBEDIENCE IN MARRIAGE

"Your desire shall be for your husband, and he shall rule over you" (Gn 3:16). From the moment of Adam and Eve's first sin, the spousal relationship has been threatened at its very foundations. Once beholding each other in a joyful "one flesh" (Gn 2:24) union, our first parents became filled with fear and distrust of one another the moment they alienated themselves from their Creator. What made the woman a fit companion for the man was her very likeness to him; though she was not his replica, he called her "bone of my bones and flesh of my flesh" (Gn 2:23). Her body revealed her likeness to him as a spiritual being, a person capable of knowing and being known by him. This truth, however, was almost immediately obscured in the aftermath of the first sin. The term "rule over" suggests that woman is now somehow beneath man, no longer his equal, no longer his partner — perhaps not so different from the rest of the material creation he is called to "subdue" and "rule" (Gn 1:28). That Eve's response was to cover her nakedness reveals that she experienced a new fear of being seen as naked: merely a body, not a person.

And so it is that throughout humanity's history, men and women have struggled, and no doubt failed, to return to the unalloyed joy of beholding one another naked and "not ashamed" (Gn 2:25). Whether subjected to the unlimited power of the Roman *paterfamilias* or even numbered among a man's property in ancient Israel, many wives have suffered greatly at the hands of husbands who held them in little esteem or who valued them only for their physical attractions, fertility, capacity for work, or social connections. And lest we think such attitudes are a thing of the distant past, only a century ago were the American "dollar princesses" married off to bail out the estates of British aristocrats; and in our own day, we witness the phenomenon of the "trophy wife" as a status symbol of men who have achieved a certain level of wealth or fame

Perhaps the prayer of Tobias in the Book of Tobit best expresses the interior struggle of husbands. On his wedding night with Sarah, Tobias begs God, "O Lord, I am not taking this sister of mine because of lust, but with sincerity. Grant that I may find mercy and may grow old together with her" (Tb 8:7). Through these words, Tobias expresses the truth about Sarah: She is his "sister," here meaning his equal, and she is meant to be valued as a whole person, not simply as a source of sensual satisfaction. He knows this deep down, but he prays for the strength to resist those post-Fall desires that might indicate otherwise. It is no accident that the story of Tobias and Sarah revolves around a demon threatening their marriage. The original source of deception in Genesis is the serpent. The serpent nudges Adam and Eve toward taking rather than receiving; his is the voice that sows doubt in their hearts about the very possibility of love.

From the beginning, God intended marriage to be a union, a "growing old *together*," as Tobias says. God did not intend marriage to be merely an instrument of pleasure or advancement for a solitary individual. Though clouded by the sins of humanity, this truth has always been understood by the inspired writers of sacred scripture. It is beautifully expressed, for example, in the Wisdom literature:

> Who can find a good wife?
>   She is far more precious than jewels.
> The heart of her husband trusts in her,
>   and he will have no lack of gain.
> Charm is deceitful, and beauty is vain,
>   but a woman who fears the LORD is to
> be praised. (Proverbs 31:10–11, 30)

These words affirm the true value of a wife for her husband, and they reaffirm the deep and abiding reality that a loving union is impossible without a disposition of trust. At the same time, they also serve to caution us wives against reducing ourselves to our charms and beauty alone.

Recall that post-Fall woman's desire "for her husband" is tinged by the same blurred vision that deceives a man into thinking that a woman is an object for his use. For women, sometimes our longing for union with a man propels us toward the false control of seduction; at other times our desire pushes us to accept treatment contrary to our dignity. A woman who "fears the Lord," however, understands her worth in relation to her Creator, who never fails to look upon her and see that she is "very good" (Gn 1:31). These lines from the Old Testament prepare the way for the Incarnation and especially for the power that Jesus Christ gives to man and woman so that both may appreciate and live up to their full dignity.

For when our Lord came, He preached a truth that puts us squarely in touch with our divine origins. When condemning the Jewish custom of divorce and remarriage, He told the Pharisees that "from the beginning it was not so." A man and his wife "are no longer two but one," according to the design of "Him who made them from the beginning" (see Mt 19:4–8). When He said that "every one who looks at a woman lustfully has already committed adultery with her in his heart" (Mt 5:28), Jesus Christ disabused his hearers of their rationalized notion of adultery as an offense against another man's "property." Instead, He penetrated to the deeper offense at the heart of such a sin: the lustful look, which reveals an objectifying reduction of a woman to a potential source of pleasure. Through his preaching, our Lord began the project of restoring man and woman's vision — the capacity to perceive reality — to what it had been at the beginning, when Adam and Eve lived in trusting intimacy with God.

Through His life-giving sacrifice on the Cross, Jesus completed this project. His grace gave man and woman the ability to achieve an even deeper intimacy with the divine through baptism — to become "like God" in a way Adam and Eve could never have imagined. As a result, the apostle Paul joyfully explains, "For as many of you as were baptized into Christ have put on Christ. There is neither Jew nor Greek, there is neither slave nor free, there is neither male nor female; for you are all one in Christ Jesus" (Gal 3:27–28). Through God's gift, we Christians experience a radically new dignity—and corresponding equality — not on our own merits but purely on the merits of divine generosity.

In celebrating what is both a restoration and an elevation to being "one in Christ Jesus," we Christians rejoice in a gift offered to all, a gift that does not distinguish between races or sexes, nor between rich and poor. Because of this liberating "Gospel innovation,"[1] as John Paul II called it, many are disturbed by any apostolic teaching that seems to hold on to the idea of "difference" in the face of equality: specifically, for our purposes, any idea of difference in the relationship between a Christian man and woman. Saint Peter proclaimed, "Wives, be submissive to your husbands, so that some, though they do not obey the word, may be won without a word by the behavior of their wives, when they see your reverent and chaste behavior" (1 Pt 3:1–2).

Although Paul began his well-known passage in his letter to the Ephesians by calling for mutual subjection between husband and wife, he followed with words similar to Peter's:

> Be subject to one another out of reverence for Christ. Wives, be subject to your husbands, as to the Lord. For the husband is the head of the wife as Christ is the head of the Church, his body, and is himself its Savior. As the Church is subject to Christ, so let wives also be subject in everything to their husbands. … This is a great mystery, and I mean in reference to Christ and the Church; however, let each one of you love his wife as himself, and let the wife see that she respects her husband. (Ephesians 5:21–33)

For so many of us today, words like "submissive," "be subject," and "head" seem utterly incompatible with the fundamental equality that Jesus offers us in baptism. Today, we as Christians often do not know what to make of such preaching. Fearing that such words undermine Christ's teachings by reflecting only the warped post-Fall relationship between the sexes, many of us simply dismiss them wholesale as being culturally conditioned by the attitudes of antiquity. Such attitudes, we assume, invariably involve embracing the domineering-male/servile-female model of family life that was institutionalized over time since the ancient world.

Could the apostles, most notably Saint Paul, have been so influenced by the household customs of their age that they would effectively have preached sin? After all, the warped dynamic of "master and slave" was a direct result of humanity's first offense against the Creator. Our modern age has virtually abandoned any "traditional" or hierarchical models of family life, in the name of woman's "emancipation" from any role in which she might be viewed as inferior. Could it be that in preaching on the submission of wives, Paul was only reinforcing the post-Fall tendencies of humankind — those of men using and controlling us women, and of us women abasing ourselves in desperation or due to reduced awareness of our own worth?

This hypothesis is not likely, particularly because the early Christians were known to be radically countercultural. Our Lord never hesitated to critique harshly the customs and attitudes of the Pharisees. Members of the early Church were set apart by their refusal to participate in pagan Roman rituals and festivals. Furthermore, Paul's words were conditioned by his reference to Jesus: Note that he implored his audience to live their "headship" and "subjection" out of a "reverence for Christ." Those words suggest that, whatever relationship he was trying to propose for couples, this dynamic was something new, part of the "Gospel innovation," *not* a reinforcing of the past.

Perhaps the best measure of how to interpret any apostolic teaching is to observe how it has stood the test of time in Apostolic Tradition: that is, the ongoing preaching of the Catholic Church. Disconcerting as some of us might find it, the idea of headship and submission — or obedience — in marriage has been preached authoritatively throughout Church history. We even find it in Church teachings from the last century and a half, most notably in the writings of Popes Leo XIII and Pius XI. In his 1880 encyclical, *Arcanum divinae sapientiae*, Leo declared, "The husband is chief of the family and head of the wife. The woman … must be subject to her husband and obey him; not indeed as a servant, but as a companion, so that her obedience shall be wanting in neither honor

nor dignity."[2]

Fifty years later, in his 1930 encyclical *Casti Connubii*, Pius XI wrote that the order of the family "includes both the primacy of the husband with regard to the wife and children, and the ready submission of the wife and her willing obedience, which the Apostle commands in these words, 'Let women be submissive to their husbands as to the Lord, because the husband is head of the wife as Christ is the head of the Church'" (Eph 5:23).[3]

These examples make clear that Paul's words were not brushed off by the Church as being insignificant products of an ancient culture. Rather, the Church has considered Paul's teaching to be essential for the establishment of the Christian family.

What no doubt needs further illumination is how to interpret such instruction, when so many today are convinced that *headship* is synonymous with *tyranny*, and that *obedience* is tantamount to *slavery*. Even the feminist movement's use of the term "women's emancipation" is eye-opening. Women in modern times — having gained the abilities to work, vote, and own property — are quite arguably more free than in past eras. But the term "emancipation" has been applied much more broadly in our culture, extending even to a woman's role in the family itself.

If women require emancipation from the community of the family, the underlying assumption is that a wife and mother is inherently unfree and should be considered less than a person.

Is it possible that the Church — charged with preaching the Good News, the truth that will "make you free" (Jn 8:32) — could get things so wrong for so long? Jesus Christ came to heal our sins and bind up our brokenness, not to confirm us in our fallen inclinations! So we need to examine more carefully the words of the Apostles Peter and Paul — those very exhortations toward headship and obedience to which the Church herself ever returns — in the hope of discovering a truth consistent with the dignity of baptized Christians, that "new creation" (2 Cor 5:17) healed of those sins that had long disfigured us. If being head does *not* mean being a tyrant, and if being subject does *not* equate with slavery, then we must seek to understand these terms in a redeemed sense — yet without a compromise that would seek to make them more palatable somehow for our times.

In the apostles' exhortations on marriage, what becomes immediately apparent is that they embraced a concept of difference even *within* the oneness (or overarching unity) in Christ that they so eloquently preached elsewhere. Instruction such as "let each one of you love his wife as himself, and let the wife see that she respects her husband" (Eph 5:33) certainly reveals an asymmetrical rather than an identical relationship between spouses. He's called to "love," and she's called to "respect"? Those two concepts alone require closer examination.

But perhaps it is most helpful to begin with a general question: Can difference ever be reconciled with oneness? Paul provides an answer in the form of an analogy. By comparing the human spousal relationship to the union between Christ and His Church, Paul gave us the key to seeing beyond a model of marriage that boils down to a mere "power play." Paul instructed husbands to "love your wives as Christ loved the Church and gave himself up for her" (Eph 5:25). How does Jesus relate to His bride, the Church? Through a gift — a gesture of offering, of sacrifice. That Our Lord "gave himself up for her" implies that our Lord is no tyrant but is rather a lover — that His headship is first and foremost rooted in His giving. A tyrant takes; a lover gives. (This hearkens back to the beginning of Genesis, when the Creator manifested His power by the act of creation itself, through the radical gift of bestowing life on everything that exists.) A husband is called to self-sacrifice to the point of death for his beloved.

That Paul called husbands to make such a sacrificial gesture for the sake of their wives should assuage the fears of many. However, this analysis does not do away with the question of what terms like "obey," "submit," and "respect" imply. Do such attitudes make a wife something like a slave, servile and unequal in dignity? Recall some of our considerations from chapter 1. A slave is one who is forced, who has not freely chosen to serve; a wife, however, is one who voluntarily chooses to submit to her husband. From the beginning, marriage included the will, the exercise of freedom. In fact, the Greek verb Paul used for "be subject" (*hypotasso*) is grammatically reflexive — it literally translates to "submit *yourself.*" He was issuing an invitation for wives to make a free choice to submit. He did not say, "Wives, you are by nature inferior beings," but rather something more akin to "You are being called to *freely make* this submission for the sake of the family."

What, then, is the exact nature of such submission? In chapter 2, we began to examine how any gift dynamic requires not one but two elements. As Catholic philosopher Kenneth Schmitz pointed out, every act of giving calls for some sort of *response*. The initial response to a gift, however, is never a return gift, for such a gesture would be premature. Instead, the primary reciprocation of a gift is the very *reception* of the gift that is offered. What does every giver hope when offering something? That the gift will be received and accepted, willingly and happily. If we give only to get something, we are not truly giving. We are rather bribing, enticing, or buying. Without someone to freely accept what one offers, the giver's gesture of gift-giving is meaningless, or at least incomplete.[4] (Consider, can one really give oneself a present? Or can an unfree creature, such as a dog, truly receive a gift? The modern trend of throwing birthday parties for pets only highlights how our culture has lost touch with the reality that only persons can truly receive gifts. The meaning of a gift — or of birthdays, for that matter — is totally lost on unfree, nonpersonal beings.) Moreover, a receiver's role is not identical to the giver's role. Yet the receiver's role is a key part of the larger reality experienced in a gift.

Let's return to Paul's teaching in Ephesians. If the husband is called to *give* himself, a wife's submission can be understood generally as a response to — a *reception* of — her husband's self-gift. John Paul II referred to a wife's submission as "above all, the experiencing of [her husband's] love."[5] In willingly receiving, in opening herself to his initiatives on her behalf, a wife is allowing him to do certain things for her. After all, how can he give his life to a wife who refuses to accept it?

Considered in this way, our role as wives seems almost easy. What person doesn't enjoy receiving a gift? Schmitz noted, however, that being a receiver is more difficult than it sounds. Being on the receiving end of a gift requires our willingness, as philosopher Gabriel Marcel described, to "accept the unexpected," a disposition he referred to as "availability."[6] After all, with a gift, we never quite know what we are going to get. How could we? One does not simply order or demand a gift according to certain specifications.

Yes, many in our culture try to do this all the time with registries, so-called gift cards, and those omnipresent Amazon wish lists (exposing yet again a spiritual poverty particular to our modern age). One reason so many today insist on more controlled forms of gift-giving is an underlying (and very real) sense that freely accepting a gift makes us quite vulnerable to the giver of the gift. To a certain degree, receiving a gift makes one freely indebted to and inextricably involved with the giver. The very word *obliged* comes from the Latin word *ligare*, meaning "to bind"; giver and receiver are bound together in a real way through their exchange. Such an involvement can be quite frightening in a world where most people want no more than they sign up for.

Thus, the receiver of a gift carries a great burden. An entire relationship can hang in the balance based upon the receiver's free response to the gift. Will she receive it gratefully or ungraciously? Will she wound the giver or inspire him to give more generously through her appreciation of his efforts? In chapter 2 we examined our first parents' resistance to receiving freely from God. The humility, trust, and vulnerability required to be on the receiving end of the Creator's gift proved too much for them. They bought into the serpent's lie that God's generosity was only His attempt to control them, not an invitation into union with Him. For gifts, offered and received, are never simply transactions; they always bring persons into a union, a spiritual connection, precisely because they require trust.[7] Persons cannot be brought into spiritual intimacy without such a risky openness to one another.

The wife's submission that Paul called for — her obedience toward her husband — begins to take on a new quality when considered as an expression of receptivity, a dynamic that goes beyond either spouse taken individually. In bringing about a kind of spiritual union that only becomes possible through the trusting interaction of two freedoms, receptivity becomes a way to understand submission that is exclusively personal and anything but slavish. Challenging, perhaps, and fraught with risk, submission understood as "free reception" becomes an intriguing concept to ponder.

That said, another question emerges as soon as we consider this dynamic of giving and receiving: the issue of mutuality. Is not love between a husband and a wife supposed to be mutual — a dual giving and receiving rather than a one-way street from husband to wife? Do we as women possess some quality that *somehow disposes us to receptivity? Do we ourselves have nothing to offer as wives?* Is a man incapable — too proud, perhaps — of receiving?

With these questions in mind, the next chapters consider insights from Teresa Benedicta and others on the unique gifts of the sexes *that seem to prepare spouses for the complementarity of a marital gift dynamic.*

CHAPTER 4

THE COMPLEMENTARY BEAUTY OF MASCULINITY AND FEMININITY

Despite Adam's description of Eve as "bone of my bones and flesh of my flesh" (Gn 2:23), man and woman, though similar, are neither replicas nor mirror images of one another. Displaying what John

Paul II called "two reciprocally completing ways of 'being a body' and at the same time of being human,"[1] man and woman seem designed to exist in an asymmetrical relationship that has often been described as "complementary." In Teresa Benedicta's many lectures on the education of women, she suggested that the physical differences between men and women are an indicator, or a symbol, of underlying spiritual differences. Examining such differences in this chapter brings much clarity to our investigation into the paradox of obedience within marriage.

If we observe our natural, physical design as women, the most obvious fact that emerges is our capacity to bear new life — our ability literally to receive and nurture another person in and through our own bodies. One might nonetheless object that human persons are more than physical beings. Is not a simple material observation an insufficient basis for making larger generalizations about us as women? The question provides its own answer: If a person is not merely physical, but is in fact a physical and spiritual unity, it does not make sense that we women would be designed with a mere physical ability to nurture persons. Reason itself demands that our design provides us with the spiritual and psychological gifts to adequately care for the new persons we conceive. (Most of us will be quick to agree that motherhood does not end in the delivery room. Rather, for most of us, the wonderful and at times terrifying journey of maternity only begins there!)

Regardless, then, of whether a particular woman ever bears a child in her life, each of us, by virtue of our female design, has been granted an interior outlook that is geared toward the development and nurture of another person. John Paul II pointed out that because women are biologically designed for such "unique contact with the new human being," we tend to manifest "an attitude *toward* human beings — not only toward [our] own child, but every human being — which profoundly marks the woman's personality." This attitude makes us, in fact, "more capable than men of paying attention to another person."[2] Teresa Benedicta commented that it is a woman's keen emotional sensitivity that makes us especially able to pay such attention to another person, to form "an understanding of the total being" of that person.[3] One glance at her child's face can often reveal more to a mother than if she were to bombard the child with questions. Many women have shared experiences of sensing what is wrong with a child even before asking. Psychologists have observed that we women:

> Pick up more on nonverbal cues and are better than men at recognizing facial differences. Sociologists have repeatedly found that women are faster and more accurate at identifying emotions. … Having the ability to pick up on nonverbal sources of information is certainly necessary to understand how preverbal babies might feel and therefore attend appropriately to their needs.[4]

So just as our female bodies are designed with "another person in mind," we find this design to be but a hint of our even broader interior ability to pay attention to and care for those we encounter.

As women, then, we seem especially designed for relationship — and even might be called "person-oriented." For many of us, this interest extends beyond babies to include kittens and puppies and plants. Helping anything small and helpless to develop is a concern that tends to come to us naturally as women. According to Teresa Benedicta, fostering the development of others is central to our feminine inclination; she noted that woman has the faculty "to interest herself empathetically in areas of knowledge far from her own concern"[5] when a matter of personal interest draws her into a situation. Venerable Fulton Sheen noted that while men tend to chat among themselves about things and ideas, we women are much more inclined to center our own discussions on other people.[6]

Are women incapable of talking about things and ideas? Of course not! We can and do — but our inclination to converse about persons so frequently does seem to reveal something about our inner nature. What we ought to consider is this: In what way is a person different from a thing or an idea?

A person is a concrete whole. There is nothing abstract about a person. When a mother takes care of her child, she does not have the luxury of caring for the child's physical needs one day and intellectual or emotional needs the next. We need to relate to our children as a whole — and in the present moment. We cannot abstract from or ignore any of their needs. Imagine a mother spending the whole day teaching her son to stack blocks or reading her daughter stories, but neglecting to change a dirty diaper. It is not uncommon for my friends and me to laugh about our husbands doing just such a thing; my husband even laughs about this tendency in himself. (Further reflection on a man's particular gifts later in this chapter and in chapter 6 will mitigate any charge of neglect against him, however.) A person is a multifaceted creature, and women are inclined and equipped to deal simultaneously with all these facets, a gift known commonly today as multitasking.

Scientific studies have suggested that women's brains are in fact wired to be more effective at multitasking.[7] Teresa Benedicta suggested that we women are natural multitaskers precisely because we are so person-oriented. We demonstrate an instinctive way of tuning in to persons (and therefore, to a multiplicity of personal details and needs) to a degree that most men do not share. Now certainly men are able — and expected — to attend to such details in life; but men tend to develop these abilities by way of learning and practice, rather than by instinct. Even those women among us who claim that they are unsuccessful at being pulled in different directions, who might fail at keeping up with multiple relationships and obligations, still seem to manifest a tendency toward multitasking.[8] The very anxiety and distress that we women often express about "not keeping up" reveals our awareness of the concrete whole, an awareness that we struggle to shed from our consciousness.[9]

If our female bodies, then, indicate not only our exterior but our interior orientation toward the human person, does this orientation imply that men are unconcerned with other people? Absolutely not. But men seem to have a less direct relationship to persons — and this distance too seems rooted in their own unique physical structure. A man's body differs from ours most notably in its size and strength. His sheer capacity for physical exertion indicates that he is designed not so much to receive and nurture a person but instead to act on the world: to work, to fight, to solve problems. And while a man certainly does this work for the sake of persons, his immediate outlook tends to be less person-oriented and much more deed- or object-oriented.

Teresa Benedicta emphasized that it is a woman's keen emotions that help us relate so naturally to persons — to sense the many needs of a single person at a given time. This is so much the case, in fact, that ignoring aspects of someone's personality can actually be quite difficult for us. Here is where we witness a difference between the sexes that again comes down to biological differences in how men's and women's brains are wired.[10] Men seem to more easily distance themselves from the details of a situation to focus on a single aspect of it or to pursue a long-term goal beyond it. Teresa Benedicta argued that this ability to zero in on some aspect of a whole informs the natural outlook of men. Another way to describe it is that a man has an ability to pursue a future goal by disentangling himself from the emotional pull of the present moment.

Many of us wives have wondered, "How can he ignore this crying baby? Doesn't he hear?" "How can he spend hours at a time watching football or playing cards or video games?" When watching football with my own husband — an interest I cultivated during our courtship due to my personal interest in *him*, by the way — I was distracted by knowing too many details about the athletes' personal troubles. When he suggested that I try to abstract a bit from their faults and focus on appreciating their athletic talent alone, I realized that he had an ability I lacked. Men often rely upon their ability to compartmentalize, shut down their emotions, and focus on a single problem to accomplish important tasks — and this can be an invaluable skill and counterbalance to a woman's gifts. On one occasion I found myself struggling with feelings bordering on resentment when my husband seemed unconcerned with our van full of sobbing children. I was struggling to keep them calm when we found ourselves stuck on a snowy country backroad. Like a lightning bolt, I realized that it was a mercy that he was able to shut them out, as his skill was required in that moment to get us out of the dangerous situation.

Noting this ability — this "masculine genius"

that we sometimes call a "laser focus" — ought not imply that men have no concern for persons, or that they do not have emotions. Most men simply tend to develop their personal skills and their capacity to relate emotionally by practice, though no doubt there are exceptional men whose abilities in this regard are more instinctual. Psychologist Greg Bottaro noted, *"A woman's body is made to make human bodies inside of her and a man's body is made to make human bodies outside of him.* The woman serves the child in proximity, while a man serves the child from a distance."[11] From a distance (however slight), a man approaches the persons in his life as a kind of project, and he employs his physical and intellectual abilities to create the conditions for their flourishing.

These complementary perspectives of man and woman, Teresa Benedicta asserted, find their source in the sexual difference. A woman's entire sense of identity is deeply connected to her body and its nurturing power. From an early age, our bodies and their natural hormonal cycles constantly remind us that we are female. We seldom feel the need to prove that we are women in the way that men tend to find ways to prove their manhood. Our bodies reveal our womanhood to us constantly; and due to this intimate link, we tend to have a certain identification with our bodies.[12] Consider the amount of time and attention we pay to the details of physical appearance as women. Our connection to our bodies can sometimes lead us toward a dangerously reductive identification with our bodies — but we will consider that in the next chapter.

A man's body-soul relationship, on the other hand, is a little less direct; his body does not immediately reveal to him that he is a man. Because his physique is designed for work, his body serves more as an instrument of his identity. Those very deeds that he accomplishes through his body form the basis for his sense of masculinity.[13] Consider the age-old and cross-cultural traditions of young men undergoing initiation rites, formal and informal, in which they attempt to prove their manhood through various actions — whether by hunting that deer, throwing that touchdown, or winning that debate.

My own husband, a literature professor, invited me to consider how much more trophy-oriented men tend to be. They do not want to settle for telling their friends that the fish they caught was "this big" — instead, they have the creature stuffed and mounted on the wall so that they can point out to all, "Look at the size of that fish I caught!" (Certainly, sometimes we women like trophies of our own. But few women see those trophies as necessary for validating our womanhood.) My husband's own PhD diploma is nailed to the wall of his office like the shield of a conquered foe. He reminded me that in classical epics, the armor and weapons of defeated enemies are incredibly important markers of achievement. In the Old English poem *Beowulf,* the hero rips off the arm of Grendel and hangs it on the wall. Things have not changed much since that was written down; men are object-oriented and see objects as symbolic of their achievements as well of their feelings. (Thankfully, usually they present flowers to show their feelings now, not the arms of monsters.)

But the masculine body-soul relationship has risks as well. A man battles against a tendency to see his body simply as an instrument he has, rather than an integral part of his identity. Whereas a woman might reduce herself to only her body, a man risks seeing his body (and hers) as merely something to use. Risks notwithstanding, the masculine and feminine orientations — toward the object and the person, respectively — complement one another. It has been said that while men tend to gravitate toward being specialists, women are the great universalists.

The fact remains that the world needs both specialists and universalists, because the family needs both. As John Paul II once proclaimed, "As the family goes, so goes the nation, and so goes the whole world in which we live."[14] The family is a reality that extends beyond either the husband or the wife as individuals; it is a union brought about only by the sexual difference. That very difference is the precondition for the new community of the family, which the masculine and feminine gifts both exist to serve. Without our sameness, our equality in our humanity, man and woman would not be attracted to one another. We would not desire to unite, and we would not be fit companions. But without our differences, it would not be *possible* for us to unite. The notion of difference emerges as something more than an "impediment to equality"; in fact, our difference is a reality at the service of a human community that both includes and extends beyond man and woman as individuals. Our difference makes us able to experience something that neither man nor woman can experience alone.

Think about that again: The family is something new — a new reality, a new union — that is only made possible by elements of both sameness and difference.

This principle finds many echoes in the teachings of Jesus. To describe the union between God the Father and humanity, He used parables filled with everyday examples of organic reality — that is, instances in the natural world that demonstrate the conditions necessary for the bearing of fruit. Consider: No earthly fruit can possibly come to be without a material coming-together, a physical union, of natural elements. Jesus gave us images of wheat and grapes, both fruits of physical unions. Wheat comes from the physical union of a seed with good soil, and grapes come from the union of a vine with its branch. In the parable of the sower, Our Lord said that the seeds that "fell on good soil and brought forth grain" (Mt 13:8) represented God's word being received by man; he said that "he who hears the word and understands it; he indeed bears fruit" (Mt 13:23). In the same fashion, Jesus described His own relationship with us as being as intimate as the vine is intimate with its own branches: "I am the vine, you are the branches. He who abides in me, and I in him, he it is that bears much fruit" (Jn 15:5). A fruit is, by definition, the result of two points of reference, two *nonidentical* elements that must come into receptive union to create the conditions for its existence. Our Lord used these visible, natural images to shed light on His invisible, supernatural union with us.

What is the nature of the spiritual fruit that we are invited to bear through such unions with God and His Word? Paul preached that the "fruit of the Spirit is love, joy, peace, patience, kindness, goodness, faithfulness, gentleness, self-control" (Gal 5:22–23). How intriguing that these virtues, these human dispositions, are described as fruit! Paul's terminology implies that such qualities are not solely the result of human effort or work. Because a union is the prerequisite for any fruitfulness, any spiritual fruit that a Christian bears is always the result of a *co*-operation. Without a seed, soil is barren; severed from its vine, a branch withers and dies. Our Lord said this clearly: "Apart from me, you can do nothing" (Jn 15:5). Without His offering, and our cooperative reception, we can do nothing.

But He did offer. The Holy Spirit was "given to us," was in fact "poured into our hearts" (Rom 5:5): a gift, a reception, something new brought forth. It is no accident that the Church, following Paul, uses a powerful image to describe her relationship to Christ: that of a bride to her bridegroom. The spousal imagery described by Paul in writing to the Ephesians revealed, *par excellence*, the way in which fruit is borne. Human persons — ourselves fruit — ideally only come about through our parents' free union, one that is both generous and receptive. A bridegroom freely offers, and a bride freely consents to be acted upon.

In this way, a physical union is transformed into a spiritual union precisely when those two freedoms are present. (Procreation is technically and tragically possible, in a physical sense, without the full consent of a woman. But such a "union" is physical only; it is incapable of bringing about that spiritual union which corresponds to the dignity of the human person.)

It therefore becomes imperative that we understand the marital gift dynamic if we are to understand how we relate to God himself. That includes understanding how the Fall of Adam and Eve created a toxic male-female dynamic that we now struggle to overcome.

CHAPTER 5

THE TOXIC DYNAMIC OF WOUNDED MASCULINITY AND FEMININITY

John Paul II described Paul's comparison of the Christ-Church relationship to the spousal relationship as being mutually illuminating.[1] Paul's analogy goes in both directions; it sheds light not only on how married couples ought to live, but also on the very way in which human persons relate to God, as "bridegroom to bride." Mysteriously, that is, the marital dynamic contains a truth about how we relate to God.

This mystery might sound exciting if it were not so confusing, for the state of too many marriages is a sorry one. Misunderstanding and mistreatment, neglect and infidelity — such painful experiences obscure God's presence to spouses more than they reveal it. The problem, unsurprisingly, is not God's design but rather the human person's undoing of it through sin. Recall that when distrust led our first parents to alienate themselves from their Creator, they deprived themselves of His enlightening friendship. They lost perspective and suddenly lacked a clear understanding of their own identities. Because man and woman are not identical, however, the sexes experienced the Fall in distinct ways. Having explored some of the ways in which the masculine and feminine orientations differ, we can now probe more deeply into the mysterious "asymmetry" of Adam and Eve's *fallen* condition.

God's admonition in Genesis 3:16–23 makes clear that the man after the Fall will be affected in his work, his distinctive mode of acting on the world.

Genesis says that the earth will now resist him and not readily be mastered, causing him frustration and exhaustion. Woman after the Fall is now similarly challenged in her particular sphere of bearing new life; she too will accomplish this work only through her suffering and anguish. These two areas reflect the distinct provinces, so to speak, of the masculine and the feminine.

But it is the relationship between the two that is now most dramatically affected because of the Fall. The reason is that each side — the man's as well as the woman's — brings distinctive gifts to the couple's union, as described in the previous chapter. When those distinctive gifts are warped by sin, they then contribute to a toxic dynamic between the sexes. Chapter 3 touched on this by unfolding the meaning of the words "Your desire shall be for your husband, and he shall rule over you" (Gn 3:16). By taking a closer look at the distinct ways in which the gifts of each sex are twisted by sin, we can better appreciate the why behind the pitfalls of the fallen spousal relationship. Why, for example, does it seem that we women are at greater risk for objectification? Why do the men in our lives seem to struggle so much with pride? A deeper understanding of such common observations enables us to return to the topic of Christian headship and obedience in subsequent chapters with sharpened insights.

Both men and women have allowed sin to affect their natural gifts — causing these good and distinctive qualities to become warped and potentially destructive. A man's particular abilities to specialize and abstract, based on how the male brain is wired (as discussed in the previous chapter), can all too easily lead him to disengage from personal relationships and cut himself off from family life even in his attempt to serve that family. How many husbands and fathers are so caught up with their work that they are barely present to their loved ones? Or perhaps they fail to understand that maintaining a family's physical needs alone is insufficient and reveals an inadequate perception of the spiritual needs of wives and children. For some men, the inner drive toward accomplishment sometimes degenerates into an exploitation of the world; drawn in by opportunities to make a profit, they fail in their duty to be good stewards of creation. For other men, work can lead to meaningless acquisition of wealth; they focus solely on money and not on the larger project of how money ought to serve the family or greater society. Worst, perhaps, is that such an ability to "zero in" on the object rather than on the person makes a man particularly prone to mistaking persons for things. The masculine gift, when weakened and twisted by his fallen desire to take, makes it only too easy for a man to view a woman as just a body to enjoy, without an emotional attachment to her whole person.[2]

Consider again that a man does not experience masculinity as immediately as a woman experiences femininity. A man's body, characterized by a unique capacity for work, takes on a more instrumental character as he accomplishes deeds through it. When he accomplishes some feat — and that feat is recognized by others — he experiences an affirmation of his person, of his manhood. It is almost as though he identifies more with the things he achieves with his body than he does with his actual body. Such an attitude, considered in itself, is not necessarily a bad thing; it can be a healthy counterpoint to that close union that we women experience with our own bodies, which sometimes leads us to overidentify with our bodies. The masculine attitude leans toward the position that the body is something "I have"; our feminine perspective is inclined to perceive the body as something "I am." Taken to an extreme, both positions miss the mark: One risks depersonalizing the body, and the other risks reducing the person to simply a body.

In truth, the body is exactly what Adam experienced when he encountered Eve. It is the symbol of the person. It reveals the human person — it manifests the presence of a creature with an invisible spiritual dimension and enables that creature to encounter others. But because the body exists in two distinct incarnations designed for union — one going beyond itself toward another, the other interiorly receptive — such a difference is clearly not only skin-deep. For the body symbolizes not just the human person in general. It symbolizes both of those necessary dimensions of a union designed to bear fruit: giving and receiving. (Recall from the last chapter that anything organic, any fruit, requires a union of two nonidentical elements: one initiating, one receiving.) This implies differences in the way man and woman approach the world from within, and consequently points to differences in the way the sexes view themselves.

It can be quite healthy for a man to draw a sense of identity from his actions and accomplishments; it reminds him that he is more than his physical dimension. But it does put him at risk of identifying himself solely with his deeds and particularly his successes, which tend to confirm his sense of masculinity. For some men, this sense can lead him to see material things — powerful or flashy cars, or the latest technological devices and the like — as markers of success. Such a self-understanding is perilous for a man because it makes him extremely vulnerable to failure, disability, or unemployment. Many men are spiritually debilitated by such obstacles because they experience in them a loss of a sense of their masculinity. (While we women might be frustrated or disappointed under similar circumstances, they do not tend to make us question whether we are women in the same way.)

Some men struggle in a particularly intense way when enduring a prolonged injury or disease. Why would the physically stronger sex suffer more than the weaker? Men are capable of incredible acts of physical exertion and endurance, but the key is found in the purpose of such actions: If a man can accomplish something through such pain (save a life, defeat an enemy, win a gold medal), it is endurable. What is much less endurable for a man is personal pain that seems useless, pain that does not seem to serve any greater purpose. A man — physically structured for action — longs for an occupation. One friend of mine, for example, goes to great lengths to contrive little home repairs that her father can work on at her house when he comes to visit — because without a project, he struggles to be at ease as a houseguest.

A man can find it equally difficult to witness a loved one's distress when he cannot find some way to alleviate it. No doubt this struggle was one reason why, for so much of human history, fathers did not attend the births of their children. Observing one's beloved in the throes of pain he cannot stop through his own effort feels like a challenge to his manhood. Interestingly, though husbands have been in the delivery room for many decades now, the current trend of women hiring doulas to support them in addition to their spouses does reinforce the idea that men tend to feel uncomfortably powerless during childbirth. Whereas doulas, usually fellow women, who regularly cope with pain that they themselves must embrace rather than remedy, do seem particularly fit to support another woman empathetically during birth. (I would not personally discourage a husband from being there; from my own experiences, my husband's presence led to bonding and greater mutual appreciation. But the increasing reliance on doulas does seem a helpful reality check to realize that husbands may not always live up to their wives' expectations during labor and delivery.)

The expectations that we women have of men might well fill its own chapter. Why does it seem that husbands are so often letting us down? Certainly, men must bear their share of the blame if they are not living up to their responsibility to love their wives (the requirements of which are explored in the next chapter). We have considered the pitfalls of a man focusing too exclusively on the object and missing the person, so to speak. Furthermore, we have examined the perils of a certain disconnect from his own body in identifying to an exaggerated degree with his work. But consider the specific ways in which our femininity is tainted by sin as well. As the saying goes, "It takes two to tango." The dance can be spoiled by mistakes on either side, and certainly by mistakes on both sides.

Woman post-Fall suffers from some complementary problems. We tend to focus too much on persons, and our identity can become bound up with our body to a dangerous degree. A woman's "genius,"[3] as John Paul II dubbed it, is our natural concern for and capacity to pay attention to persons. Although a man might sometimes be oblivious to others because he is absorbed in a project, it is rare that we women are not noticing people.

What happens to that attitude when it is wounded by sin? One obvious warping of our predisposition is when our predisposition degenerates into unbounded concern with the business of others. Women at our weakest gain a sense of importance simply through involvement in the juicy details of other people's lives. Sound familiar? That women are most often the perpetrators of gossip is no accident. It is a perversion of our natural interest in persons. Sometimes this concern propels us to insert ourselves into the lives of others and draw satisfaction by clinging to those who "need us."

Furthermore, because of our gift of multitasking, we can too easily make the mistake of dabbling in too many activities or relationships at once, putting ourselves in danger of living only at a superficial level. Where a man might get lost in a project, we women sometimes have our hands in so many things that we find it difficult to enter very deeply into anything.

Perhaps the greatest source of struggle for the feminine soul affected by sin is dealing with our source of strength: our ability to relate emotionally. Without deliberate self-control, however, a woman's emotions can become her worst enemy. It is all too easy for us to become obsessed with relationships and to become slaves to our feelings. As Alice von Hildebrand puts it, "If all the tears shed by women had been collected since the beginning of the world, they would compete with the sea. The tears shed by men might fill a pond of modest size."[4] This is not to suggest that all tears are bad — in fact, they are a tangible sign of human sensitivity. But it is healthy for each of us to reflect on how many times our own tears may have been shed out of self-pity, self-centeredness, wounded vanity, or taking things too personally. Perhaps worst of all are the tears we have shed over imagined offenses.[5] We women have an uncanny ability to create fantasy worlds.

Teresa Benedicta proposes a good reason for this: Women, as mothers, need to be able to use our imaginations to recognize and develop the potential in our children. But the very essence of recognizing potential consists in being able to see something that is not actually there yet — to anticipate. As part of our wounded nature post-Fall, women sometimes see things that simply aren't there at all, and will never be there. We may find ourselves feeling snubbed when perhaps we are not; we may perceive drama that is really only coincidence; we may read far too much into what others say or do.

Combined with these tendencies is our underlying identification with our female bodies. Because our bodies so regularly remind us that we are female, we sense a kind of body-soul unity, which can be quite healthy. We are much less at risk of seeing another person as an object — we instinctively sense that another body is always in intimate association with another person. Furthermore, we do not as easily fall prey to the same fear of failure that men experience, because we do not tend to identify with our work in the same ways they do. In most women's minds, I am distinct from what I do; a man finds this distinction more difficult to make. (It may be worth noting, however, that many modern women do tend to experience greater anxiety about professional failure than in past eras, no doubt a product of decades of education emphasizing performance and career placement. Aspirations toward motherhood — or even professions which engage a more typically feminine orientation toward nurturing and relieving personal needs — are regularly dismissed as "aiming low." Consistently directing women toward paths valued only for their pay scale has played a pivotal role in causing women to undervalue their natural feminine strengths.) Such a trend is perilous, because, like the masculine sense of identity, our feminine sense has its own weakness: that of feeling so closely *connected* with our bodies that we simply *identify* with them. Woman post-Fall risks reducing herself to her physical attributes alone, to seeing herself as "just" her body. Obsession with body image — though not exclusive to women — is directly related to a desperate fear that one's worth lies only in one's physical desirability. Plastic surgeries, exercise fanaticism, fad diets, eating disorders, so-called slavery to fashion: So many of us succumb to the lie that our value is exhausted by our bodies rather than revealed through them.

Considered individually, these warped versions of masculinity and femininity are frustrating to behold. But taken together, they constitute the foundation for a truly poisonous dynamic — one we see described succinctly in the third chapter of Genesis, when the Lord declares to Eve: "Your desire shall be for your husband and he will rule over you" (Gn 3:16). Now that we have reflected on the natural asymmetry of the masculine and the feminine, the fact that sin places us in a particularly vulnerable position as women is no longer such a mystery. The man ruling over the woman in a dominating way is a result of how sin has warped his masculine gift. Instead of giving himself to her, the man will be inclined to take from the woman as though she were just another object. His capacity to block out emotion sadly assists him in this approach to the woman.

That the woman does not always resist such

treatment suggests that her own personal orientation—her own desire for relationship, her longing for
another person—is a driving force behind her way
of relating to the man. Struggling with her own reduced sense of identity, she tends to seek affirmation
in his eyes. Directed by her emotions, her "desire"
for him seeks his attention and acceptance. Looking
to the man to fulfill her sense of worth, the woman
post-Fall places herself under his power, even though
she sought to avoid what she suspected to be God's
control. With such an ugly backdrop of men and
women relating as master and slave, it is no accident
that so many of us recoil at the Church's teaching on
a wife's "obedience."

In his work *Love and Responsibility*, Karol Wojtyla (later John Paul II) called the woman, whose
"desire shall be for her husband," a victim of "pure
sentimentality."[6] Person-oriented by nature, emotionally hardwired for fostering relationships, she
now craves such relationships at any cost. Woman
post-Fall finds herself prone to romanticizing and
overidealizing the opposite sex, often to her own det-
riment.

Recall that it is women's natural gift to be able to
recognize potential in others; but that gift is transformed into a liability when it becomes unhinged

from reality to such a degree that we sometimes see qualities in men that are not there. When we perceive a "real discrepancy between the ideal and the reality,"[7] we risk disillusionment and even misery. Driven by our desire for emotional gratification from a man, we struggle with *waiting to receive a gift.* We women want that personal connection so much that we can become willing to compromise our very identity and can sometimes struggle to see ourselves as more than a body, even risking objectification.

John Paul II refers to our counterpart, man, after the Fall — he who would "rule over" us as women and view us merely as potential objects of sexual satisfaction — as suffering from "pure sensuality."[8] In a sad complement to the woman, who struggles with waiting to receive his gift, the man post-Fall finds it nearly impossible to give that gift. Already object-oriented by nature, he struggles to distinguish the woman from among the world of objects and might attempt to use her accordingly. His longing for sensual enjoyment is so strong that it can inhibit his freedom to give — his ability to master his desires — and instead inclines him to take what he can.

In both cases, man and woman after the Fall tend to overlook the full reality of one another and consequently lean toward a depersonalization of one another in relationships. In their work *Called to Love*, Carl Anderson and Jose Granados noted: "Whether we identify love with the sexual impulse like the man or with dazzling emotions like the woman, in either scenario we tend to treat this reduced version of love as an absolute that forces itself upon us and deprives us of any free initiative."[9]

It is clear that sin warps the spousal relationship by threatening the freedom of man and woman — specifically, the freedoms to give and to receive that ensure the fruitful gift dynamic between ourselves and our husbands. We must understand how the sexes are affected by sin if we are to distinguish their dysfunctional relationship after the Fall from the new relationship proposed in the New Testament. There, Paul defines a man's headship as a sacrificial giving, and he defines a wife's submission — by extension — as being lived through grateful reception.

Having explored the deep, gender-specific wounds within the heart of man and woman affected by sin, we can now consider the ways in which Jesus Christ proposes to heal those wounds. What we will discover is that Paul's words are just the prescription for restoring man and woman to authentic mutuality and true intimacy.

CHAPTER 6

HEADSHIP ACCORDING TO CHRIST'S IMAGE: HUSBAND AS "GIVER-IN-CHIEF"

What Saint Paul seems to be asking of married couples is that they work to undo the damage wrought through original sin. *Undoing* is a theme Saint Paul emphasized when he taught, "By one man's disobedience many were made sinners, so by one man's obedience many will be made righteous" (Rom 5:19). If giving until the bitter end is what Our Lord calls husbands to do when they hear "love your wives, as Christ loved the Church and gave himself up for her" (Eph 5:25), no doubt Paul intended to counteract those fallen inclinations to "take and enjoy" that have plagued men — and injured women — throughout time.

By the grace of the Holy Spirit poured out by Jesus' sacrifice on the cross, a husband is strengthened and enabled to fulfill his masculine genius by serving as "giver-in-chief" of his family. It is no accident that the creature whose unique design equips him to act, to perform deeds, on another's behalf is the one called to "give himself up" for his wife. As we considered in chapter 4, men find a deep interior satisfaction when their actions or accomplishments are recognized and valued by others. In this chapter, we look at the design of man more closely as a way to understand why men are called to headship according to Christ's image.

Men are designed to give and, perhaps more importantly, are designed to experience personal fulfillment in doing so. The question remains, however, as to why such a generous posture is referred to as "headship." Headship is synonymous with authority. So many of us in modern times equate authority with tyranny, a force that imposes and robs its subjects of their freedom. Such a characterization, though influenced undoubtedly by the bad examples of those who have sinfully abused authority throughout time, is not accurate.

Consider the word *authority* itself: The root is *author*, coming from the Latin *auctor*, meaning *source*. Indeed, what is an author but the very source of a thing's life? An author brings a thing to life. The philosopher Yves Simon described the function of authority in a similar way, though from a more political perspective. He argued that authority was an essential principle in governing people, because every group of people needs guidance and coordination if the common good is ever to be achieved. He claimed that the precise function of authority is to "vivify" each of the different parts of a whole.[1] And what does *vivify* mean? To energize or bring to life — there is that idea again. True authority brings out the life of those it serves.

When Paul uses the analogy of a head and body ("for the husband is the head of the wife … husbands should love their wives as their own bodies" [Eph 5:23, 28]), he is undoubtedly referring to the same life-giving dynamic. A head serves and coordinates the members of the body so that they will be healthy and fully functional. Yet it is not, in actuality, separate from that body. Here we see another biblical comparison to organic unity: Head and body are, in a living person, "one." Paul said, "For the body does not consist of one member but of many. ... If all were a single organ, where would the body be? As it is, there are many parts, yet one body" (1 Cor 12:14, 19–20). The good that the head serves is the good of the body of which it is a part. The common good that a person in authority serves is his own community, that larger reality which extends beyond him but also includes him.

A head that abuses its body, therefore, cannot help but harm itself as well. When those in authority — in the political or the domestic sphere — misunderstand their role as tyranny, they attempt to dominate their subjects. This tyranny crushes their spirit, drains them of life, and in so doing makes of itself something monstrous. All authentic authority must be true to its name: It must foster life.

A husband is called to foster the life — both physical and spiritual — of his wife and children. In preaching to the Ephesians, Saint Paul's use of the head-body image reminds us that any true authority must serve its community, its body, through sacrificial gift. His words did not define a new kind of headship; rather they served to distinguish what characterizes true headship from false and destructive versions. To be head in the manner of Christ himself is, in fact, a return to the concept of authority as life-giving power that we find in the creation accounts of Genesis. There, all that *is* comes into being through God's gift. How, then, does Jesus Christ give life to the Church? By pouring out His life for her in a sacrificial offering. "Giving life," then, is no mere metaphor! This principle was affirmed by John Paul II, when he stated that in "revealing and reliving on earth the very fatherhood of God, a man is called upon to ensure the harmonious and united development of all the members of his family."[2] Through his initiative and purposeful activity, a husband's project is to realize the potentialities of those under his charge — to foster their life.

A husband's works — these gifts, so varied in kind — are the concrete manifestation of his authority, his life-giving role in the family. The *Catechism of the Council of Trent* phrased it in this way: "The husband should … constantly be occupied in some honest pursuit with a view to provide necessaries for the support of his family and to avoid idleness, the root of almost every vice."[3] "Honest pursuit" — a husband's work, by which he materially supports his wife and children — is one of his primary gifts to his family. Such efforts typically exhaust the majority of most husbands' time and energies. It is through such endeavors, however, that a husband creates the conditions for his family to flourish by attending to their many material needs.

One might wonder: Does such an obligation on the part of a husband preclude his wife from supporting the family through work outside the home as well? It does not, and chapter 8 is dedicated to understanding how spouses can live headship and submission in the context of varying employment situations today. Nonetheless, we must take a moment to consider just how a husband is to view his material support. If he is to truly foster life, his efforts must always aim at empowering his loved ones, freeing them in some way to fulfill their capabilities. (The root word of *potential* is *potens*, meaning powerful.) He must free his children to develop their potential. One example is a child's need to learn the value of hard work. How many fathers labor to give their children everything and end up depriving them of opportunities to learn the value and satisfaction of working to earn something themselves?

And that means a husband's labors must free his wife in some way. His efforts must enable his wife to fulfill her *person-centered* nature, to cultivate the emotional ties upon which she and her children thrive, and to use her specific gifts for nurturing those lives. Though a woman's interior gifts for nurture and personal attention are instrumental in serving many beyond the home, they are specifically oriented toward her own children first and foremost.

What this implies for a husband is that his work is in no way limited to a nine-to-five job, assuming he works outside the home (see chapter 8 for a discussion of different family situations). Rather, his gift to his family must include his assistance with domestic chores such as cleaning, cooking, and laundry — anything that helps his wife to be more patient, nurturing, and attentive toward their children. Wives who also contribute to the material support of the home through paid work especially require such assistance from their husbands — but it is critical to clarify that a wife who stays at home requires help too! The notion that all domestic work is somehow the province of women ignores the basic principle of a husband's headship. He is there to give, in whatever way he can, to support the persons he loves. Such support invariably takes different forms; but if he approaches the family as a project for which he is responsible, he will be anything but idle in his efforts.

This project, though material, is not simply material. So all of his actions must take into account not only the physical but the spiritual flourishing of his family. A supportive husband will work to find a solution when the mother of his children is becoming depressed or overwhelmed. Whether he pitches in more around the house, works longer hours to pay for extra assistance for her, or simply takes her out on a date, maintaining her emotional well-being falls under his authority. Emotional availability is another, sometimes difficult, area of his gift to her. For many men it takes a certain effort to be wholly present to another — it is so easy for a man to become too focused on something that distracts him from what matters most (particularly in the age of the smartphone). Moreover, attentively listening to his wife's thoughts and feelings, particularly if they involve worries or anxieties, can be difficult for a husband, because his instinct is to solve problems, not simply to provide relief by being a good listener. Such support, though challenging for many husbands, is an invaluable gift to a wife.

Teresa Benedicta also recommends that a husband work to support his wife spiritually by encouraging her to participate in creative activity of her own. A husband, the saint says, is responsible for the consequences "should he try to confine her [his wife] to a sphere too narrow for her talents."[4] Most wives I know need little encouragement in this area. We don't have to be convinced that our hobbies are worthwhile; we just require the time and opportunity to engage in them! Already juggling a myriad of responsibilities, many of us often make such activities a low priority. We push them off to another (mythical) time "when things aren't so busy." Our husbands' efforts to carve out these creative outlets for us is critical in making them happen. They do need to push, sometimes, to make sure that we do prioritize them; they need to offer time, energy, and enthusiasm to create such a space for us.

For some women, a husband's enthusiastic attitude is most valuable. His enthusiasm can remove (irrational) feelings of guilt that wives and mothers sometimes carry when we do something just for fun, "just for me." In fact, a good husband can only reap the reward of a happier wife if he makes these efforts. Recall from our reflections in chapters 4 and 5 that our feminine gift of multitasking sometimes makes us prone to more superficial forms of engagement. Add our wounded tendency to sometimes place more value on our physique than on our accomplishments. When a husband makes sure that his wife can nurture her hobbies, his encouragement can go a long way in helping her maintain her sense of self-worth. And by reminding her that she is more than her body, a husband expands his wife's sense of spiritual identity in a healthy way. Though every woman's life has more intense seasons (for example, when our children are young), a loving husband will make an effort in this regard, however modest.

Another form of spiritual support that a man offers his family is in the area of education. John Paul II's encyclical *Familiaris Consortio* states that a father's "more solicitous commitment to education" is a "task he shares with the mother."[5] A son learns most effectively from his father that men who are true to their vocation do not mistreat women. A son learns he must not abuse his strength by showing disrespect to the women in his life (beginning with his mother and sisters and extending to all women he encounters in the public sphere). A son also gains a better sense of his own masculinity when his father is attentive to and encouraging of his own budding projects and achievements. And from her father, a daughter learns in a unique way a sense of her own dignity, particularly when his attentions to her are not limited to her physical beauty. The way a husband treats his wife profoundly affects a daughter's sense of her own worth and likewise establishes her expectations of her future spouse. In each case, a father educates his children in these principles most powerfully by his own example of faithful love toward their mother. His educative presence makes a tremendous impact upon his family, and this factor ought always to be considered when he finds that his job is taking him away from the family too often.

A necessary feature of a man's educative contribution to his family is a disposition of gentleness. What some well-meaning fathers fail to understand is the degree of power that is rooted in their presence alone (not surprising, as men tend to identify more with their actions or words). When men regularly use a harsh tone or rely too heavily on corporal punishment, they can stoke an unhealthy fear in their families. Paul is careful to remind them: "Fathers, do not provoke your children, lest they become discouraged" (Col 3:21). Children are extremely sensitive to the attentions of their fathers and naturally seek their approbation. So when fathers are overly critical, they can crush their children's spirits, thus debilitating that development that the father is supposed to serve. This warning is not to suggest that fathers must avoid being firm, especially in matters of discipline; but a key factor seems simply for him to pay attention. Particularly in the age of internet technology, a man finds it all too easy to be physically present but spiritually absent from his family. We wives — with our acute sense of personal presence — can be an effective aid in reminding our husbands to notice our children. The more a father is fully present, the less he will find that he needs to use unholy fear to guide a child. Because children approach their father with a kind of natural awe — a healthy response to his size and strength — he can better inspire and guide them with his natural gifts by being intentionally present, versus resorting to tactics which prey only upon their fears.

One might object that such examples — this nonexhaustive list of instances of physical and spiritual support of one's wife and children — are generally expected of a good husband and father. The material point here is that such activities are essentially an exercise of true authority. We shouldn't view them as threats to our dignity as wives, nor as part of an outmoded paradigm of marriage.

What usually causes discomfort for modern couples when addressing the topic of husbandly authority, however, is the area of decision-making. Does a husband's headship extend to decision-making? Certainly, we cannot deny that each member of the family has a proper sphere of activity, in which free decision-making is possible and necessary. How can anyone be prepared for a fully human life if his or her freedom has not been developed? A tyrannical husband and father reduces his wife and children to slaves who operate out of fear. In such cases, they are stunted in their spiritual development, which he has failed to promote.

Spouses, as a natural part of their vocation to love, should seek to communicate as openly as possible regarding decisions that affect their family's future — and should seek consensus. Pope Pius XI clearly pointed out that a wife's call to submission in no way implies that our free decision-making ought to be curbed — as a child's is curbed at times, due to ignorance or immaturity.[6] In fact, a wise husband often heeds a wife's advice and defers to her expertise in many matters — particularly those regarding our children, to whose needs, feelings, and moral development she is particularly sensitive.

But every family goes through times when the husband and wife cannot reach a consensus. How does a Catholic couple proceed? As mentioned in chapter 3, Pope Pius XI taught us that the "order of love" of the "domestic society … includes both the primacy of the husband with regard to the wife and children, the ready subjection of the wife and her willing obedience."[7] Understanding the family as a kind of natural order, the Church has identified a husband's "primacy" and a wife's "obedience" as essential principles of that order. Pius XI continued:

> This subjection of wife to husband in its degree and manner may vary according to the different conditions of persons, place and time. In fact, if the husband neglect his duty, it falls to the wife to take his place in directing the family. But the structure of the family and its fundamental law, established and confirmed by God, must always and everywhere be maintained intact.[8]

Pius XI understood that headship and submission will vary to a degree, as times and situations change. But he was firm in asserting that the structure of the family demands that such an "asymmetric" dynamic exist for the good of the whole. Put simply, it makes sense that someone in a family, for practical purposes, should have a final say that allows the family to function when it cannot reach a consensus. Both Scripture and Church tradition place that responsibility on the husband.

But is it biologically true that a man is somehow more suited to such a role? Can those typically masculine gifts described in chapter 4 somehow prepare him to wield such a responsibility in a way that is superior to how we might wield it as women? Psychologist Greg Bottaro noted that biology may offer support for such a position:

> There is less connectivity between the right and left hemispheres in the male brain. This allows for greater *compartmentalization*. At the same time, there is actually more connection between the front and back of each hemisphere in the male brain. These two realities contribute to the masculine genius. Men are better at spatial organization and abstract thinking, both of which utilize intra-hemispheric communication. These qualities dispose a man to make decisions and solve problems that are related to the external environment. Intra-hemispheric frontal-lobe modulation is more natural for men, which makes it easier to detach from the emotional considerations of a situation.[9]

What does this mean? It means that a husband's ability to "zero in" and abstract from the pull of emotions can assist him in situations where clarity is blurred due to strong feelings surrounding an issue. Recall also that a man tends to be future-oriented; we women, because of our attention to persons, are at times so consumed with tending to them in the present moment that we can find it difficult to abstract from a situation in order to gain perspective. The capacity to abstract from the particulars of a situation in order to consider the concept of what is good for the family as a whole is a masculine gift which the husband is to place at the service of the family.

The above reasoning, however, may still seem somewhat shaky. What guarantee do we have that in a given situation the course of action we propose as a wife would be less wise than a husband's? Happily, another reason supports a wife's deferring to her husband when the couple has reached a stalemate. This reason has nothing to do with a man's strengths, and everything to do with a woman's. Teresa Benedicta reminds us that our nature as women gives us a distinct advantage in accepting our husbands' decisions in difficult matters. Why is this so?

The feminine ability to subordinate our own interests for the sake of a personal relationship[10] enables us to get on board more easily with decisions which we may question. As we touched on in chapter 4 — and will explore in greater depth in chapter 7 — Teresa Benedicta noted women's special ability for "empathetic interest" in areas "far from [our] own concern," which assists us in making a personal connection to others. When my mother was dating my father, for example, she learned everything about cars to get closer to him. I learned about football so that I could have an excuse to hang out with my future husband on Sunday afternoons. Another mother I know — having only male children — has become an expert on all things military in order to bond with her sons. Because we have such a deep-seated orientation toward persons and relationships, we tend to give those relationships top priority — even if that prioritizing means we stretch ourselves to appreciate things toward which we might not otherwise be inclined.

For this reason, I have come to appreciate the characterization of Elastigirl, the mother of Pixar's *Incredibles* family. A wife and mother's superpower does seem to be that of being stretched and pulled, expanded and expended, to meet the many needs of our loved ones. While this superpower does not imply that we find it easy to accept a spouse's differing decision, it does suggest that we women have a certain power to subordinate our own preference to his decision for the sake of our spousal relationships.

How would a man do in this kind of subordinating role? Being object-oriented, a man tends to focus more exclusively on the problem and struggles more to accept a decision with which he does not agree. He tends to concentrate so wholly on the issue at hand that he is generally less capable of entertaining personal considerations. (Recall that a man tends to identify with his actions — including decisions — thus tying himself to them in a way distinct from what we do as women.) So when I as a wife insist on my way, I take a very real risk. Should my decision backfire, my husband may be less willing to take responsibility for its consequences.

He lives his headship most authentically, then, when he possesses a disposition of responsibility and accountability for his family's flourishing. If the decision, however flawed, is his, he is more motivated to own it and to make it right when things go wrong, being bound to his actions in his distinctively masculine way. Furthermore, my ability to stand with him as a wife — because I can more clearly distinguish my love for him from my opinion of his decision — provides much-needed support in these situations. Together, the complementary gifts of husband and wife give couples the capacity to maintain family unity and to weather the storms that never fail to accompany family life.

What is important to keep in mind here is that these types of final-say decisions should not be the norm in a healthy, sacramental marriage; they ought to be the exception. Those who argue against a husband's authority often paint a picture of a dictatorial husband making final decisions on a daily basis, while his passive, subservient wife keeps her opinions to herself. Such a couple is in need of an intervention! Healthy, honest communication is critical to keeping decision impasses at a minimum — and couples should never shy away from seeking counsel if they are struggling in this area. I often advise my female students to think twice before marrying any young man who seems overly keen on asserting himself as head of the house. Such a position can be quite burdensome, because a husband must make decisions for the common good of the family — not to satisfy his own whims as titular household head.

I once spoke with a woman whose parents had recently weathered a significant storm. Her father had opted to accept an early retirement package, buy and build on a large property, and invest what remained in a new and promising business venture. His wife was opposed. She did not think he would be happy retiring so soon, and she was concerned about the investment risks. She was honest and vocal about her objections, but he was convinced his plan was for the best — after all, he wanted to please her and build her dream house! She submitted, and they went through with the plan. Shortly after building the new house and a beautiful barn, his investment venture collapsed. He was forced to reenter the work force and was unable to keep up on necessary maintenance on the new buildings for nearly a decade. What could have broken his spirit was only a glancing blow, however; his wife's love and tenderness toward him under these disappointing circumstances were precisely what motivated him to keep going for so many more years, working hard (at the expense even of his health) to make it up to her. When their daughter told me this story, she described them as having an incredibly happy marriage. Her mom's strength in allowing her dad that fateful "final say" decision was her expression of unity that ultimately motivated him to "keep on" giving until they reached a better place.

When pondering the burden of decision-making, I am reminded of a fictional marriage that falls under the category of a "cautionary tale": the

Bennets of Jane Austen's *Pride and Prejudice*. Mr. Bennet believes that it is imprudent to allow his flirtatious young daughter Lydia to go on a seaside holiday to Brighton, unsupervised by her family. But he refuses to insist that she remain at home, being instead worn down by Lydia's — and more so, his wife's — constant pleas that she be allowed to go on this trip. He gives in to the ladies' desires, then, not out of a regard for what he thinks is best but only to avoid unpleasantness. He admits that "we shall have no peace at Longbourn if Lydia does not go to Brighton."[11] Too weak to endure the disappointment and continued complaining of his wife and daughter, Mr. Bennet abdicates his role as head of the family. Unsurprisingly, when this choice that he did not make (but only failed to stop) backfires and Lydia elopes with an unsavory young man, Mr. Bennet still does not heartily step up to take responsibility. Instead, he is driven further away from his wife in the fallout, even as he is mortified by his own weakness in failing to stand up to her.

How many husbands and fathers today bypass head*ship* because it can be such a head*ache*? Too many men are willing to take the path of least resistance because they would rather not be the "bad guy," particularly when it comes to saying no to their children's wishes. When husbands "check out" in such a way, I cannot help but recall the desperate words of Elastigirl to her oblivious husband, Mr. Incredible, as their children's fighting descends into chaos: "Bob, it's time to *engage*!" Being willing to engage means being willing to lead, even at the risk of making a mistake. The universal truth revealed in the example from *Pride and Prejudice* is that avoiding the responsibility of headship means eclipsing the possibility of unity. The Bennets are driven further apart and experience only suffering in their marriage. The real-life couple who lost their retirement, however, was able to stay united and happy — even in spite of misfortune — because there was headship and submission, risk and receptivity, in their married life. It was painful but ultimately fruitful, because only true unions can bear fruit, and only giving and receiving can create a union.

Headship, then, requires strength because it entails risk and responsibility, and these can be daunting. Those men seriously contemplating marriage who do not experience some trepidation at the prospect are simply not prepared for headship. (Add the fact that Paul presents Jesus Christ, God Incarnate, as their model to follow in assuming such a role.) But lest a man despair of living up to the divine standard, another human inspiration for living authentic headship can be found in Saint Joseph. Though one opinion holds that Joseph's initial response to Mary's pregnancy — that of resolving "to send her away quietly" (Mt 1:19) — was fueled by his belief that she had been unfaithful, another interpretation is particularly encouraging for husbands.

Aquinas described how some of the Church Fathers believed that Joseph's decision was motivated by something altogether different:

> But according to Jerome and Origen, he had no suspicion of adultery. For Joseph knew Mary's chastity; he had read in the Scriptures that *a virgin will conceive* (Is 7:14), *and there will come forth a rod out of the root of Jesse, and a flower will rise up out of his root* (Is 11:1); he also knew that Mary was descended from David. Hence he more easily believed that this had been fulfilled in her than that she had fornicated. And therefore, considering himself unworthy to live with such great sanctity, he wished to hide her away, just as Peter said, *depart from me, for I am a sinful man, O Lord* (Lk 5:8). Hence he did not wish to hand her over, i.e., to take her to himself,

and receive her in marriage, considering himself unworthy.[12]

This line of reasoning suggests that Joseph attempted to exit the stage not because he considered Mary unworthy, but because he considered himself unworthy to step into the holy drama that was unfolding. Being asked to enter a role for which he felt unprepared and undeserving: this sums up the fears of many husbands. Joseph did not think he was holy enough, perfect enough; yet to be Mary's husband and foster father of Jesus Christ was what God *asked* of him. Note that the angel tells Joseph in his dream, "Do not *fear* to take Mary [as] your wife" (Mt 1:20). Fear is the response of the humble to the holy. Mary, too, experienced it at the Annunciation when she was invited to become the mother of God.

What underlies both accounts is that Mary's receiving and Joseph's self-offering are both expressions of obedience. For a man to embrace the role of head is an act of obedience to God. His wife is most certainly not the only one called to obey here. John Paul II told us that "Joseph *obeyed* the explicit command of the angel and took Mary into his home, while respecting the fact that she belonged exclusively to God."[13] Here we see that true headship is a service, one that demands more than what seems humanly possible. This truth is why we must reflect on Gabriel's words reminding us that "with God nothing will be impossible" (Lk 1:37). John Paul II summed up the essence of real authority when he wrote, "Through his complete self-sacrifice, Joseph expressed his generous love for the Mother of God, and gave her a husband's 'gift of self.'"[14] What a model for all husbands!

CHAPTER 7

SUBMISSION AS AN IMAGE OF THE CHURCH

We now face the task of interpreting a wife's obedience as a form of receptivity. For if true authority is generous, true obedience seems to require gratitude. We first pondered the words of John Paul II in chapter 3: "a wife's 'submission' … means above all 'the experiencing of love.'"[1] After considering the many ways in which husbands are called to love us through acts of giving, we might be inclined to wonder if our only role as wives is to be a grateful receiver of such gifts? Even those occasional "gifts" in the form of decisions with which we didn't agree in the first place? Furthermore, does such an attitude define or exhaust our capabilities — have we nothing to offer as wives and women? At the outset, any wife can find the concept of obedience to her husband a bit hard to accept.

It is helpful initially to recall our considerations of masculinity from the previous chapters. Because of a man's tendency to identify with his work, we noted, his own sense of manhood does not develop automatically. Rather, it seems to grow over time as he accomplishes deeds that are recognized by others. When his father or another boy at school praises a young man for an accomplishment or admires something he says or does, that young man experiences an affirmation of his identity. When what a man does is well received by others, the term *respect* usually describes the attitude with which he is met. And so men tend to think of respect as something they earn through deeds well done.

But is not respect, then, synonymous with appreciation or gratitude? When one is pleased with a gift received, one is grateful. Moreover, if a man identifies with his actions, he himself feels "well received" when those actions are met with respect. While a man may attempt to demonstrate love through acts of giving, he himself experiences love by being received. A man feels loved when what he does is appreciated.

Consider again Paul's words: "Let each one of you love his wife as himself, and let the wife see that she respects her husband" (Eph 5:33). The husband is called to "love" and the wife to "respect"? Does not a husband wish to be loved? Is not love mutual? Hopefully it is becoming clear that the mutuality of love contains within itself the very asymmetry of the gift — always two points of reference, the giving and the receiving, which correspond (surprise!) to the distinctive orientations of the masculine and the feminine. In other words, for a man, "respect" translates to "love"!

So in contrast, as women, designed biologically and emotionally to receive, we desire love in the form of a gift. We long to receive; we want to be given gifts. To be clear, the notion of a gift is not restricted to some item that comes wrapped with a bow on top. Any generous — that is, freely initiated — gesture offered for another person's benefit rises to the definition of a gift. When we receive a generous offering from our husbands, we feel loved. Paul's words reflect the truth that men and women tend to experience love differently. A woman craves love in the form of a gift; a man craves love in the form of her gratitude for his gift.

But this observation again raises the question of mutuality. What does a wife have to offer? And how does a man receive? Well, we wives certainly perform countless gifts of service to our families each day. The deeper question, though, is whether our gifts, our offerings, succeed in making our husbands feel loved. No amount of doing on my part will make my husband feel loved, if I am not at the same time expressing gratitude for *his* gifts. The most capable and generous wife in the world will have a miserable husband if she shows no respect for him. In fact, she could hardly be called "generous," because her greatest offering to her husband is something she is denying him: that respect he so craves.

A wife's ultimate gift is no *thing* at all, then — rather, it is an attitude of appreciation. The mutuality is there; but it is subtle and asymmetrical. A marriage therapist confided in me after one of my lectures that of the hundreds of couples he had counseled in his career, not a single husband said he felt respected by his wife. Noting this fact is not to assign blame to the wives in those sessions (for who knows how many were being mistreated?), but simply to illustrate that if respect is not present in a marriage, the couple is not experiencing mutual love.

This dynamic was not immediately obvious to me in my own marriage, but after a while I gained insight in reflecting upon something as mundane as Christmas shopping. For many years I wondered why it was so difficult to find the perfect gift for my husband (or for my own father, for that matter). Though my husband always noted my thoughtfulness in choosing a gift for him, over time I came to realize that, deep down, what made my husband most happy at Christmas was when I was thrilled with the gifts he presented me. That response made him feel loved.

By using this example of Christmas presents, I am not trying to restrict the notion of gift-giving to material offerings wrapped and presented formally. The exchange of tangible presents simply captured for me in a clear way what the men in my life desire. It is a simple truth that though a man is pleased to receive offerings from his wife, what he most craves and what makes him feel loved is her own delighted response to him — to what he offers her. Such a response is her gift to him. Our *admiration* for what our husbands offer us — their handiwork, ideas, and opinions — can mean more to them than all of the labor we ourselves put into family life.

So a woman sensitive to a man's soul knows that an appreciative manner can truly build him up and inspire him to become even better. Just as we nurture others in our lives, we must make room to receive and appreciate what our husbands have to offer.[2] In fact, it is difficult to put into words how inspiring a wife's appreciative manner can be to a husband — as well as how deeply his own sense of identity is affected by his wife's confidence in him. This in no way implies that we women do not also deserve gratitude — we absolutely require respect in our relationships. But we usually distinguish respect from love in a way men do not seem to do. I do want my husband to appreciate me, and I do deserve his respect — but I still want him to bring me flowers, take me out to dinner, and rub my feet. For me, respect is not a substitute for love. Gifts mean love to me, as much as appreciation and respect communicate love to him. And again, giving can be expressed in many forms, as articulated in the very popular book *The Five Love Languages*.[3] Ranging from the conventional "item with a bow on top" to quality time, from affirming words to acts of service and physical touching — all gifts contain some visible or sensible element but also always symbolize something deeper. A gift is always a concrete manifestation of one person freely offering himself to another. So consider each of the different ways a husband lives his headship, as described in the preceding chapter. Each of these ways of being "head" is to be considered a gift; each gesture of physical and spiritual support for the family is a tangible sign of a husband's self-offering. This truth sheds light on a woman's craving for gifts as well. What we are actually longing to receive is the person that the gift represents. Our person-oriented nature shapes the way in which we experience love.

But if love is supposed to be mutual, how does a man receive love that we offer in turn? That most men feel somewhat uncomfortable owing another person is no secret. Witnessing a group of men vying to outspend one another at a charity auction revealed to me that not an insignificant amount of pride is bound up in a man who identifies with being a giver. Certainly one might argue that the wish not to be beholden can counteract laziness by motivating a man to work hard to earn a living — but such an attitude is not without risk. For it is just such a pride which makes men resistant to receive charity when their families fall on hard times.

We women seem especially designed to assist

men in this area. Physically weaker, much more accustomed to depending on another for support (particularly when our energies are consumed with bearing and nurturing children), and quite familiar with enduring pains outside our control, we can serve as a reminder to the men in our lives that their fundamental status is that of creatures: beings whose very existence has been given to them by the Creator. Alice von Hildebrand commented, "Women definitely have an advantage over the strong sex because it is easier for them to acknowledge that they are weak and depend on divine help."[4] A wife is one who can prompt her husband to remember that he is not the ultimate Giver — and perhaps more importantly, that his ultimate worth is not dependent upon his own successes or failures, but instead on that Giver's love for him.

So although husbands can cling to their identity as givers and sometimes struggle to receive well from others, they do have a more natural way of demonstrating their reception, though their way is more subtle. By acting as chief giver, a husband demonstrates *his* gratitude, his appreciation for his wife, *through* those same acts of giving, much in the same way she gives back to him through her manner of receiving. It is an honor for him to be able to give to her, to have his gestures of offering recognized and cherished exclusively by her. Remember, one cannot be forced to accept a gift; the very root of gratitude is *gratis*, meaning "free." A husband's outgoing deeds (in all their different forms) demonstrate his gratitude for his wife. It is a gift to him to be able to bestow something upon her. Consider the phrase "allow me," which we say when performing a service for another. A man gets to have his offerings (and in reality, himself) accepted by a grateful wife — it is his privilege.

Preserving this dynamic of thoughtful giving and grateful receiving is critical to the health of our marriages. Such a dynamic can be a bit more challenging, but equally essential, when we women take on the role of materially providing for our family; the next chapter illuminates the path to giving and receiving even within more modern scenarios of family life and financial support.

Regardless of the specific details of a family situation, however, our submission in marriage is powerful. Responding to a husband with respect affirms his identity and, as a result, builds his confidence. For the greatest risk for a giver is that one's gift will be rejected. Fear of failure or rejection runs deep in men, and hopefully by now we clearly see why this is so — for it is not really the gift we are spurning when we are not pleased with what he offers, but the man himself.

The problem is this: What are we to do when our husband does not get it right? Affirming a husband by grateful submission can be extremely difficult. The very nature of a gift is that it is given, not ordered. Husbands, though they act in the image of Christ, are imperfect and can easily disappoint us, despite their best efforts. How can we wives respond with appreciation when a husband refuses to give, or when he does not give well?

St. John Chrysostom tells us that "a wife should respect her husband even when he shows her no love, and a husband should love his wife even when she shows him no respect."[5] Is Chrysostom suggesting that we ought not tell our husband when he is not serving us or the family well? No, he's not saying that — but it behooves us to tell our husband with tenderness, by finding something to praise, something to be pleased with, even while trying to gently express what we need from him. After all, a husband who fosters the life of his family should be always seeking to know what his loved ones need. Ultimately, because he is a giver, his greatest desire is to make his family happy, starting with his wife. He cannot fulfill this role without humility on his part — a willingness to change if he sees that his wife is not wholly pleased. But when we try to communicate our needs through harsh confrontation or sarcasm, we can find that our efforts have the reverse effect.

By now it is apparent just how powerful a wife's obedience is during those occasional final-say decisions. When we stand with our husband out of love for his person (rather than his decision), we give him an incredible form of support. Should his decision fail somehow, he will not be crushed by it because he is not alone in it. Moreover, he will be more motivated to do better in the future because of the gratitude he feels to us for sticking with him. And if he were loath to take our advice in the first place, he might be more open to that in the future, too.

Another way in which we wives sometimes achieve the reverse effect is by presenting our husband with all our needs and worries at the same time. One young mother I know was so accustomed to overloading her husband with requests and anxieties upon his return home each evening that he developed a habit of stopping at a nearby park just to collect himself before the encounter. Recalling that a man's special ability is to abstract from the whole in order to focus on a single problem, we wives are wise to recognize that bringing every concern simultaneously to our husband is bound to distress him, as well as confuse him about what we want him to prioritize. We do well to make time for even brief moments of prayer and recollection before such conversations, if we are striving for healthy and fruitful communication with our husbands.

Approaching a husband with kindness as well as calmness when trying to communicate our needs — particularly needs that he perhaps has failed to meet — is not easy, but it is necessary. The extreme alternative to respecting a husband who fails to give well is simply to make demands. The most obvious problem that arises with this model for marriage is that it is a documented failure. The example of the fictitious Bennets mentioned in the previous chapter suggests just how much damage is inflicted on a marriage when a wife insists upon having her way against all of her husband's objections. God's design seems to have ordained it this way, as the very idea of making demands erases the freedom of a husband's gift, dealing a blow to his sense of manhood, which is bound up in being a giver. Harsh criticism from a wife is poisonous to a man and thus to their marriage. It can seriously compromise his ability to give, because his identity is wounded by our digs at his efforts. Here lies the deeper problem: Without the confidence borne from our admiration, our husband can become paralyzed by fear of failure. If he's always wrong and we're always right, why bother trying? A husband will tend to shut down then, becoming a shadow of a man, and his wife will remain unsatisfied because she will not feel loved *unless* he takes a risk.

Only through beauty, admiration, and gratitude is a man truly motivated to continue giving. When we show appreciation for his deeds, however imperfect, we are communicating a respect which affirms him to the core. Even Saint Peter seems to touch on this truth when he says that husbands who "do not obey the word may be won without a word by the behavior of their wives" (1 Pt 3:1). A wife's delicacy, her respectful adherence to her husband, is often precisely what has awakened in many a husband the vocation to live as another Christ. For every husband fails in some way — and though she may be tempted to do so, no woman should respond to the failure of a husband by failing as a wife.

Does St. John Chrysostom's advice apply to a wife whose husband is abusive? No, it does not. While some degree of neglect (a lack of affection, insufficient material provision) might be addressed through a spouse's gentle and loving motivation, abuse — that is, cruel treatment, emotional or physical — cannot be endured without causing deep spiritual injury to all members of the family. Gratitude is reserved for gifts; abusive words or physical injuries are the opposite. They do not enrich, but rather attempt to rob us of our dignity, which is essential for us to maintain not only for ourselves but for the sake of our children. Pius XI was clear when he proclaimed that no wife is bound to obey her husband's request if it "is not in harmony with right reason or with the dignity due a wife."[6] A wife in an abusive situation is bound to remove herself and seek help because it is essential that she preserve her dignity — already fragile in a woman, who is more inclined to have a reduced sense of personal identity. The husband, for his part, can only hope to overcome his sins in this regard if his wife refuses to tolerate them. Though such situations are tragic, are often complicated, and require much support from beyond the family, we must understand that submission to abuse is not true submission, because it is rooted in fear rather than freedom.

In a related way, it is important for all women to know when we ought to refuse to submit. One common example of a request contrary to our dignity is when a husband insists that his wife use contraceptives. How many husbands justify this request out of a purportedly prudential concern for family size? Such a request does not call for our obedience, however, because it does not reflect the appeal of a true authority. Recall that any exercise in headship, any display of authority, is always associated with a gift, a sacrifice. When a man is unwilling to deny himself the marital act during the woman's fertile times — when he instead asks her to jeopardize her physical health and psychological wholeness so that he may enjoy her without taking responsibility for the life she may conceive — he is no longer a giver but a taker, one who objectifies his beloved. If he is ever to exercise legitimate decision-making authority in this area (or any other), his authority must always involve selflessness on his part, with a regard for the integral good of his loved ones. Sacrifice is always the hallmark of true headship, which is why natural family planning (NFP) is the only acceptable Catholic approach to avoiding a pregnancy. It requires a husband and wife to deny themselves the marital act out of respect for one another's integrity — a challenge requiring communication, discipline, and strength. Hard-won virtues, to be sure, but a boon to every marriage!

Yet some wives, perhaps ignorant of or feeling overwhelmed by the prospect of NFP, resist the very idea of resisting such a request. How many of us contracept out of fear that our husband might not rise to the challenge of exercising periodic abstinence? "What will he do if I'm not always 'available'? What if he turns to someone else, or to pornography? Will he be angry if I do become pregnant?" we may wonder. Perhaps we feel, as Eve did, that we can really manage things better on our own. (Recall that Eve was alone when the serpent approached her and tempted her to take the shortcut to wisdom.) Perhaps we believe that we can achieve what we want without being vulnerable, not trusting that our husband could ever face the challenges asked of him.

What we wives need to remember is that, more often than not, our husband's ability to do something depends heavily on whether or not we have confidence in him! An etymological root of confidence is *fides*, meaning faith, or trust. Without a generous giver and a *trusting* receiver, there can be no gift. Without gift, there can be no love, and without an environment of love, human persons — men and women — start to lose their humanity.

CHAPTER 8

MODERN APPLICATIONS OF HEADSHIP AND SUBMISSION

Though I have described material, financial support for a family as one concrete expression of a husband's sacrificial headship, providing such support is not limited to a husband. In our current age, many of us wives are employed outside the home, in addition to or instead of our husbands, in jobs both full-time and part-time. The reasons for such arrangements are numerous, emerging from many factors that influence the economics of family life. Rising costs of living, the spouses' relative employability and earnings levels, and college debt are only a few of the reasons that might motivate a wife to work outside the home. Recalling that Catholic couples are called not only to procreate but also to educate our children, many wives work to enable our children to attend (always expensive) Catholic and private schools. Some of us work because our husbands suffer from poor health, physical or mental; others because we possess a unique talent or skill that serves the larger community in a vital way. Still other wives may choose to work because of a special passion for our field, from which we draw inner peace and satisfaction.

Again, the reasons are perhaps as numerous as the situations. The critical issue for this reflection, however, is that such arrangements do run the risk of blurring or obscuring the way in which a husband lives his authority, his headship, and how a wife lives obedience in response. How does a husband foster family life through his efforts if he is not the only (or even the primary) material provider? And how does his wife show him submission if she is the breadwinner (or one of them) for the family?

One reminder from chapter 4 sheds light on this question: Namely, a man tends to approach the persons in his life as a kind of project and directs his energies, physical and mental, to create the conditions for their flourishing. Zooming out from the specifics of breadwinning as such, a husband's project thus includes evaluating the overall functioning of his family. If he assesses, in consultation with his wife, that the family's overall good — physical as well as spiritual — is benefitted by his wife working outside the home (in addition to, or instead of, him), it becomes his role to do whatever he can to support such an arrangement.

Not surprisingly, supporting such an arrangement requires the mark of any true headship: sacrifice. Such headship may mean (and has any wife ever not appreciated?) providing more assistance with housework and meals and making more efforts with the children. Some husbands inadvertently refer to spending time alone with their children as "babysitting." Though we wives may tease them over this kind of remark, what the term sometimes signals is the husband's underlying sense that, for him, child care and home care are temporary arrangements, a desperate way to hold things together until the mother comes home. A husband and father who embraces more hands-on home duties on a permanent basis is obliged to go further — to strive for excellence — whether in managing domestic life or in seeking to understand and nurture his children better. Though many women have an advantage intuitively in these provinces, a motivated man can excel by learning and practice.

Beyond offering this very practical assistance to create the conditions for his wife to maintain a job, a husband must continually assess the mental health of his loved ones as well. If he observes that his working wife is experiencing burnout or is stretching herself too thin, it is his place to work toward a change. Such a change no doubt will require him to sacrifice more. He may have to give even more of himself to relieve the pressure on his wife. In certain circumstances he might be called on to give up his own job and stay home with the family, if he discerns with his wife that her job is essential for the family's thriving. Such changes are costly for a husband — they sometimes involve surrendering his preferences for a nicer house, car, or vacation. They may involve directly taking on the education of his own children through homeschooling. What these changes always involve is a selfless assessment of what is best for his family as a whole, followed by a willingness to respond with action and creative adjustments when problems arise.

In chapter 6, we examined some ways in which a husband is called to support his wife spiritually to enable her to find time to engage in hobbies and creative outlets that enhance her own happiness and sense of self-worth. For some of us wives, a paying job may be the outlet from which we derive this sense. One woman may find joyful fulfillment from doing a job well. For another woman, the desire to work may come from a different source: Some of us, due to life experiences (including but not limited to loss or abandonment), deeply fear being solely dependent upon a husband financially. Others of us struggle with the prospect of full-time childrearing; we have anxiety (sometimes shaped by our own childhood experiences) about failing in some way with such a heavy responsibility.

For women in all these situations, sharing in or fully taking on paying work outside the home — work in which we find greater self-confidence — is a way to maintain our inner peace and stability, which benefit our family overall. At times, creating the conditions in which we may work outside the home *is* our husband's form of spiritual support for us. In no way does it preclude him from praising and encouraging us in our motherhood as well, of course, should we struggle with confidence in that area. Consistent words of encouragement and affirmation are an extremely valuable gift to any wife, naturally.

One caveat, however, concerns a wife who works outside the home for pay to relieve an inner pressure or fear. Specifically, her reasons (and their family dynamic) may be unhealthy if her primary motivation is a lack of confidence in her husband's ability to provide. No doubt some situations warrant such a fear, and it is appropriate for a wife to take this step to provide for the family. But in other circumstances, she might instead be suffering from a trust issue, perhaps due to previous wounds or possibly due to a particularly anxious temperament. If a wife experiences such a fear — such a struggle to trust in her husband — and insists on working for pay, her marriage risks becoming a minefield of mutual resentment: she ultimately resenting carrying the load, he resenting her lack of trust in him. (The latter can be experienced in a particularly acute way, given a man's perception of work as an expression of his identity.) If a husband's support for his wife's career is to be genuinely fruitful and life-giving for his marriage and family, his support must presuppose his wife's own trust in his love and care for her, no matter what form such care takes in a given situation. Anything less risks undermining their marriage itself.

Because a husband is oriented toward the overall good of the family, at times he must risk upsetting his wife (something no husband desires!) if he observes that their children are suffering in some way due to her work situation. He must be courageous enough to communicate his concerns to her and to pitch in, in whatever way, to help address the issue. Conversely, he must be ready to respond with action should his wife express a desire to return home, or if she should observe that his own career is taking a negative toll on the family. Each situation is unique; one universal factor is the husband's viewing of the family as a project to support. His special ability to approach it as such a project must work in concert with his wife's special ability to anticipate the needs of her children. And a wife's submissive response to such a communication, while difficult, will call upon her deepest instincts of attending to the needs of the persons in her life and of subordinating her preferences for the sake of her relationships with them.

Having examined what form a husband's gift takes in the complicated arena of providing for the family, we need to take a closer look at its counterpoint: how we wives live our grateful acceptance of such a gift in these scenarios. Just how a wife expresses such a reception — particularly when she herself is in a position of supporting her family, in whole or in part — can be challenging. A man who does not earn money (or all the money) may find it difficult or awkward to give his wife gifts (in the conventional sense of material presents), especially if she manages the budget. And she may find it just as challenging to express gratitude when she is financially supporting the family.

Although it is certainly appropriate for the husband to show appreciation for his wife's efforts, just as she would show gratitude for her husband's gifts, such is not sufficient for spouses to affirm one another at the deepest level. What this situation requires is a determined effort by husband and wife to affirm one another according to the natural ways in which each one longs to be loved.

What does that mean? A wife (who feels cherished by receiving a gift) needs to be especially attentive and make an effort to recognize and to affirm the work of the home that the husband has taken on to enable her to maintain a career. This affirmation can be tricky if she herself is very capable in the domestic arena. If she is overly critical, is eager to show that she knows best, or reveals a lack of confidence in his abilities to care for the home or the children, she risks wounding him, for his very identity is bound up in such work, as always. For his part, a husband must see to it that his wife feels cherished; he must find ways to be a giver, even if it calls for him to think outside the box: mastering a recipe and preparing her a meal, renovating or repairing something in the home, helping the children to make her a gift, or arranging a babysitter and surprising her with a night out.

Here let's reaffirm that not all gifts come to us wrapped with a bow. Though many of us long to be brought flowers or taken out on a date, other women crave gifts in other forms. Some of us desire our husband's attentive (technology-free) presence and sympathetic ear; others, a simple hug! Sometimes we just want a respite of time alone, to reflect or to pursue a hobby. Some of us desperately yearn to pursue an activity with our husband, or as a family. One friend of mine absolutely loves going on dates with her husband to Lowe's and picking out items for home projects. Some of us simply desire that our husband help with chores without being asked.

Spouses must make efforts to learn one another's "love language." It is often astounding to see how many years a couple can be married and still be fairly oblivious as to what really pleases one another. And though the responsibility goes both ways, a husband who is fulfilled through gestures of giving would do well to really understand what delights his wife. In some situations we women are "bringing home the bacon," but we still desire deeply to feel cherished by receiving gifts (cloaked in many forms) from our husband.

Corresponding to this gesture of gift-giving, then, is that we wives must have the acuteness to recognize and appreciate a gift when it is given. Some husbands do consistently give in less obvious ways and are hurt when we do not receive those gestures with appreciation. We need to be attentive and expressive of that gratitude which is so inspiring to the men in our lives. It is all too easy for a wife to feel neglected, and for her husband to lose self-respect, if spouses do not understand the underlying dynamic that makes love possible. Concrete situations may change from generation to generation, but the union that spouses experience will only remain strong and healthy if it is marked by the asymmetry of giving and receiving which established it from the beginning. For couples, the task of navigating such situations is a complex one which requires healthy communication skills — and discernment in prayer.

Why prayer? Prayer helps us prioritize those dimensions of the human person that our culture tends to ignore. Opening the consideration of career choices to a divine perspective is key in a culture that emphasizes material fulfillment above all else. We must keep before us the truth that "man shall not live by bread alone" (Mt 4:4). It can be too easy to prioritize physical needs and comforts over the emotional and spiritual benefits gained by time and presence together as a family.

In chapter 2, we reflected upon the original symbolic power contained in the human body to make Adam and Eve spiritually present to one another, capable of real intimacy. Our modern obsession with more disembodied forms of social communication has obscured the power of families spending real time together in one another's actual presence. In an age when an online culture wields more influence in many children's lives than their parents do, both fathers and mothers in all situations are called to reconsider the value and power of their bodily presence and time in forming the character and self-image of their children. Inviting God into this consideration of just what Catholic couples wish to bestow upon our children will help ensure that our efforts are not one-sidedly material and will, in fact, take into account the emotional and spiritual development of all members throughout the varying seasons of family life.

CHAPTER 9

THE POWER OF OBEDIENCE

Frankly, the state of marriages today suggests that good spouses are indeed hard to find. We must keep in mind, however, that just as the toxic dynamic between husbands and wives is the result of sin, the new Christ-Church dynamic can only be the fruit of grace and of each partner's transformation through a baptismal relationship with Our Lord. We must never forget that — as we touched on in chapter 3 — Paul prefaced his declaration of the spousal dynamic of love and respect with the words "Be subject *to one another* out of reverence for Christ" (Eph 5:21, emphasis added). What John Paul II referred to as a "mutual submission"[1] between the spouses does not, however, negate the asymmetry in their relationship. Instead, he insists that each spouse find the motivation to relate to the other in a "holy fear of Christ" — an attitude that is not fright, but rather "reverence for holiness."[2] Each spouse is called to make his or her unique contribution to marriage an expression of personal love for the Lord.[3] Connecting our earthly marriages to himself through the shedding of His blood, Jesus, according to Pius XII, "sweetened any taste of bitterness" that we wives may experience. He wrote that Our Lord showed how the authority of the head and the submission of the wife can, without losing anything, be transformed by the power of love, a love which imitates the bond which unites Him to His Church. He showed how constancy of command and respectful obedience can and must, in an active and mutual love, achieve selflessness and a generous reciprocal gift of each other.[4]

The concept of "reciprocal gift" has been key in this book for developing our understanding of the nature of the spousal dynamic. For though the word *reciprocal* tends to be used synonymously with words such as *mutual* or *joint*, a kind of unevenness or asymmetry is built into the notion of gift, as we have noted. Giver and receiver are not identical; they do not perform the same role. A giver freely offers something. In fact, when presenting a gift to someone, a giver is indeed offering more than simply that item, whatever it is. Any gift, however small or large, symbolizes the giver. (We know this instinctively, because when our own gifts are rejected, we ourselves suffer as the giver.) When that gift is received, then, the giver is the one who is spiritually accepted into relationship by the receiver. Schmitz calls the formation of this invisible bond the "metaphysics" of a gift. The husband, as giver, wants the receiver to "have him"; when the receiver accepts, she is consenting to such a wish. She wants what he wants for her.[5]

What becomes clear in this close examination of the marital relationship is that such reception is a distinctly personal act. It is not mere passivity; rather, it requires our openness to another and our disposition of trust, which is only possible for a free creature. Our decision to respond with gratitude to our husband's gifts can be excruciating at times, but it is precisely in such moments that our status as free creatures is most remarkably expressed. The determination to smile when disappointed, the decision to be gentle when he's made a mistake, the choice to stand with him in a decision: In each situation, our dignity as persons radiates, because no lower creature could bring about what we do through such receptivity.

And what does such receptivity accomplish? It, and it alone, brings about spiritual unity. Persons can spiritually unite; they can belong to one another — and gift is the only path by which they bring it about. As philosopher Damian Fedoryka points out:

> We can possess another person more intimately and thoroughly than we could ever possess what is normally called *property*. And the reason for this is that the other person can give himself or herself to us. … We have the capacity to take possession of our being so that we can give ourselves, for nothing can be given to another unless it first belongs to the giver. Because God created us for himself, He gave us to ourselves.[6]

Such is the very purpose of our freedom — so that we have the power to give ourselves to, and to receive, one another. When we receive our husband's self-offering as a wife, we are "opening the door" and allowing the interior belonging that only personal beings can experience. What power is to be found in receptivity! Consider the way in which our appreciative attitudes affirm our husbands' identities and build their own self-confidence: Such is the direct result of the unity — that oneness and fortifying solidarity — that we make possible through our receptivity.

Why so much emphasis on receiving rather than on giving? Surely the call to sacrificial gift is a heavy and heroic one for husbands! The first reason is to undermine the common misconception that submission is dehumanizing and weak. We have probed the concept and found that submission is both uniquely personal and incredibly powerful. The second reason is because, whether male or female, we all locate ourselves squarely in the position of receiver in the Church. In our relationship with Jesus Christ, we are the Bride. Obedience is our role. Putting obedience into the new light shed by our submission as wives can only help us all know better how to achieve union with the Divine.

Our Lady demonstrates in a singular way the unity made possible through obedience. As chapter 1 alludes, she achieved a total union with the Holy Spirit through her acceptance of the invitation to become the mother of God. What makes her reception, her obedience to God's will, so singular is her sinlessness. Sin, by definition, is wanting something that goes against the will of God. As Catholic apologist Frank Sheed explained it, Mary, being sinless, did not desire anything apart from the will of God. So, because she did not give over any of her being to what is not God's will, she was able to exhibit a singular feat: Mary was able to receive God perfectly. She received with the entirety of her being, not holding anything back for herself alone (which is always what sin is — wanting something just for me that God does not wish for me).[7]

That such a perfect union took place is evinced by the fruit that was borne from it. Recall our reflections that fruit can only emerge from a union — it cannot come about without a receptive element. Mary's words say it all: "Let it be to me according to your word" (Lk 1:38). Allow me to paraphrase her: "Lord, I want what you want for me. I accept the gift you are offering me *and the union with you that my consent makes possible.*" Such is the very definition of accepting a gift. Uniting one's will with another's will is a free act, and *it creates union.* For our will, our freedom, is a spiritual power; making it one with another's will is the definition of spiritual union. Just as two persons who suddenly understand the same truth are brought closer together, two persons who choose the same good are spiritually bound. Mary's union with the Holy Spirit is so perfect, so complete, that it brings forth divine fruit.

Mary's consent to the divine will did not end at the Annunciation. As Federico Suarez wrote, Mary "did not love Jesus at the expense of or above the will of the Father. On the contrary, she loved and accepted the will of the Father even at the cost of her Son."[8] Such a cost, such a suffering, is often compared to the sufferings that Jesus himself endured. St. Alphonsus Liguori wrote that "In the death of Jesus, Mary united her will to that of her Son in such a manner that *both offered one and the same sacrifice.*"[9] Echoing this point, Suarez noted that "The union between Jesus and Mary was such that Simeon's prophecy was no mere metaphor."[10] Suarez's implication, no doubt, is that the same lance that pierced Jesus' side simultaneously pierced Our Lady's soul. The total trust demonstrated in Our Lady's perfect reception of the Holy Spirit at the Annunciation made her especially vulnerable. Mary was so united to her Son that they suffered as one.

Such a oneness resulting from acceptance of the divine will is found not only in Mary, but within the depths of the Holy Trinity. In a heartbreaking expression of obedience to His Father during his agony, Our Lord manifested the very unity of the God-head. For in His anguish in Gethsemane, He prayed, "Father, if you are willing, remove this chalice from me; nevertheless not my will, but yours, be done" (Lk 22:42). Not my will, but yours. Jesus united His human will with the will of His divine Father; He, like Mary, embraced the Father's will for Him. And what do we know about Jesus' relationship with His Father? He tells His disciples, "I and the Father are one" (Jn 10:30). Accepting another's will for us — receiving what that other wants us to have — unites persons, even Divine persons!

What is essential to note here is that such unity does not preclude bitterness. Sometimes what we are asked to accept, to receive as what "God wills for us," is painful. But our Lord, in unitive obedience to His Father, drank His own cup to the bitter dregs.

As members of the Church, we are all invited into union with our Bridegroom through obedience. Our ready embrace, our free acceptance, of God's will for us is the gateway, the opening to union with Him. Detaching ourselves from sin is the challenge, for we are fallen creatures, still bearing our wounds and weaknesses even after being baptized into Christ's Bride, the Church. When we grasp at those things that we desire but that God does not desire for us, we take a tremendous risk. For as Sheed reminds us, sin is an effort to gain something against the will of God; "but the will of God" he wrote, "is all that holds us in existence; when we sin, we are hacking away at our only support!"[11] Like our first parents, who took rather than received, we lose rather than gain when we sin, because we cut ourselves off from our source. We inhibit union with God and others when we sin, and we succeed only in isolating ourselves. We keep God at a distance, but He alone can lead us — through a union with Him — to become like God.

The challenges of married life — or any other vocation, for that matter — can only be endured if they are understood through the greater lens of how we receive God's will for us through the events of each day. A difficult wife who does not affirm her husband, a distracted husband who is insensitive to his wife's feelings, an irritable religious superior who does not seem suited to his or her position — each might make us despondent unless we have subordinated every relationship to our primary one: that of obeying God through our chosen vocation, sufferings and all. If we give ourselves over to our own role, and work to detach ourselves from our own sin, we will experience a deepening union with God that will assist us in enduring the inevitable heartaches in this Valley of Tears.

Whether we are married or not, each of us is meant to be touched by marriage, for we are all born into a family. We are designed to arrive at an understanding of ourselves and our Creator in the context of such a community. When generous gift and grateful submission establish a profound unity in earthly marriage, we are given a glimpse of the Trinity as well as of the relationship between Christ and His Church! Whether our particular vocations are characterized by the generous reception of Mary or by the self-gift of Joseph, each is a form of obedience to the saving plan of the Gospel, which brings woman and man back into that communion from which they were torn through distrust.[12] As Saint Augustine wrote, "He who created us without our help will not save us without our consent."[13] *Obedience* is another name for our consent, and it is the only thing standing between ourselves and Divine Union. Perhaps Dante says it best in *The Divine Comedy*, when he attempts to describe the essence of heaven through the character of Piccarda Donati, who explains to the Pilgrim:

Indeed the essence of this blessed state

Is to dwell here within His holy will,
So that there is no will but *one with His* [emphasis mine].[14]

But lest our identity seem to be absorbed or negated by such oneness, we must recall Mary's words at the Visitation, just after she entered into her own union with the Divine: "My soul magnifies the Lord, and my spirit rejoices in God my Savior, for he has regarded the low estate of his handmaiden. For behold, henceforth all generations will call me blessed" (Lk 1:46–48). Mary standing before Elizabeth is filled with joy! She is not diminished by freely choosing to receive God's will — she is completed. Elevated from lowliness to blessedness, Mary experiences the way in which a union makes a person more than she could ever be alone. Mary was given to herself, so that she could offer herself and experience beatifying union with her Creator. Her obedience — her receptivity — opened her to what was considered impossible. Such is the ultimate truth about the human person, and it is indeed good news.

ACKNOWLEDGMENTS

Though short, this book is the fruit of decades of study, prayer, conversation, and lived experience. There are so many persons to whom I owe thanks, and I am sure I would always leave someone out if I tried to name them all. Nevertheless, I must mention a few personally: Dr. Janet Smith, Thomas Mirus of *The Catholic Culture* Podcast, Mary Beth Giltner of OSV, and Fr. Donald Planty for their encouragement of this project; all of my professors at the John Paul II Institute and Dr. Damian Fedoryka for their wisdom and guidance; my colleagues and students at Christendom College and my wonderful siblings, in-laws, and friends for their support; and, of course, my husband and children: Trey, Lucy, Tommy, Beatrice, Jimmy, Jack, Caroline, and Bertie. None of this could have been accomplished without your love, patience, and encouragement. (And I have wondered more than once if a woman with such an ideal husband really has any business writing a book on marriage …). Last, I would like to thank my parents, Jim and Dorothy Amorella, and my in-laws, Tom and Gemma Stanford, who have given me more than I could ever repay.

NOTES

CHAPTER 1

1. Sir Francis Bacon, *Novum Organum*, ed. by Joseph Devey (New York: P. F. Collier, 1902), Bk. I, Aphorism 98.

2. Joseph Cardinal Ratzinger, *God and the World: A Conversation with Peter Seewald* (San Francisco: Ignatius, 2002), 106.

3. Ratzinger, *Introduction to Christianity* (San Francisco: Ignatius, 1990), 41.

4. Ibid., 25.

5. Ratzinger, *God and the World*, 106.

6. *Catechism of the Catholic Church*, 2nd ed. (Washington, DC: United States Catholic Conference, 2000), 863.

7. I am indebted to Damian P. Fedoryka for his insights on this simple but profound distinction,

which may be found in his essay "The Dignity of Man and the Dignity of Knowledge," *Faith and Reason*, Vol. XIII, No. 1, 1987. One confusing factor here is that people do "blame" their pets all the time for misbehaving. Such a response on our part, however, is really an example of anthropomorphizing our animals, or ascribing human traits to them. In truth, if our animal acts in a way we do not desire, we can only blame ourselves for placing it in circumstances which happened to trigger a deeper instinctual urge.

8. Thomas Aquinas, *Summa Theologica*, 2nd rev. ed., trans. Fathers of the English Dominican Province (London: Burns Oates and Washbourne, 1920), I-II, q.6, a.5.

9. Maximus the Confessor, *The Life of the Virgin*, trans. Stephen J. Shoemaker (New Haven, CT: Yale University Press, 2012), 50.

CHAPTER 2

1. John Paul II, *Man and Woman He Created Them: A Theology of the Body*, trans. Michael Waldstein (Boston: Pauline Books and Media, 2006), 13:3.

2. I am indebted to Kenneth Schmitz for his insights on the dynamics of a gift found in *The*

Gift: Creation (Milwaukee: Marquette University Press, 1982), 48. We examine these further in chapter 3.

3. John Paul II, *Man and Woman*, 26:4.

4. Ibid., 27:4.

5. Ibid., 13:1.

6. Ibid., 27:4.

7. Carl Anderson and Jose Granados, *Called to Love: Approaching John Paul II's Theology of the Body* (New York: Doubleday, 2009), 115.

8. John Paul II, *Man and Woman*, 32:6.

9. Edith Stein, *Essays on Woman*, 2nd edition, revised. Vol. 2 of *The Collected Works of Edith Stein*, trans. Freda Mary Oben (Washington, DC: ICS Publications, 1996), 72.

10. Ibid.

CHAPTER 3

1. John Paul II, *Mulieres Dignitatem*, August 15, 1988, Vatican.va, par. 24.

2. Leo XIII, *Arcanum divinae sapientiae*, February 10, 1880, Vatican.va, par. 11.

3. Pius XI, *Casti Connubii*, December 31, 1930, Vatican.va, par. 26.

4. Schmitz, *The Gift*, 50–51.

5. John Paul II, *Man and Woman*, 92:6.

6. Gabriel Marcel, in *The Philosophy of Existence* (1954), as quoted in Schmitz's *The Gift*, 48.

7. Schmitz, *The Gift*, 49.

CHAPTER 4

1. John Paul II, *Man and Woman*, 10:1

2. John Paul II, *Mulieres Dignitatem*, par. 18.

3. Stein, *Essays on Women,* 74, 96.

4. Greg Bottaro, "The Female Brain: What's Your Superpower?," *CatholicPsych Institute*, January 21, 2020, https://www.catholicpsych.com/blog/the-female-brain-what-s-your-superpower.

5. Stein, *Essays on Women*, 46.

6. See Fulton Sheen, *The World's First Love* (New York: Garden City Books, 1952), 134.

7. Psychologist Paul C. Vitz cited a variety of studies to suggest that a woman's ability to multitask is supported by the wiring of her brain. Vitz explained that a woman has more lateral connections across the *corpus callosum* — that is, across the right and left hemispheres of her brain — than does a man, whose mental processing is usually confined to one hemisphere and even there tends to occur within localized regions or "modules." Vitz suggested that this difference is why men tend to become more irritated when

interrupted than women do. He observed that men "need to travel a longer internal neural distance to address the interruption as well as to escape from their focus in a particular task-based module. For women, crossing the corpus callosum is much easier, and being less module-based…[they] can more quickly move from one task to another even if they stay in the same hemisphere. Dealing with family life and dealing with people demands easily coping with interruption and not showing irritation or hostility." Paul C. Vitz, "Men and Women: Their Differences and Their Complementarity: Evidence from Psychology and Neuroscience," in *The Complementarity of Women and Men*, edited by Paul C. Vitz (Washington, DC: The Catholic University of America Press, 2021), 205.

8. Neuropsychiatrist Louann Brizendine noted that in the eighth week in the womb, baby boys receive a "huge testosterone surge" which effectively shrinks their centers for communication and processing of emotion. Infant boys tend to focus on objects — mobiles, lights, and doorknobs — while baby girls gaze much more exclusively at faces. "Over the first three months of life, a baby girl's skill in eye contact and mutual face-gazing will increase by over 400 percent, whereas face-

gazing skills in a boy during this time will not increase at all." Louann Brizendine, *The Female Brain* (New York: Morgan Road Books, 2006), 15. Vitz noted that this female inclination toward faces is sign of a woman's "people skills." He wrote that "women have better memories for *episodic* events — that is, private events usually involving persons and their activities and interactions with others." Vitz, *Complementarity*, 200.

9. Brizendine noted that a woman's "intense sensitivity" toward those in her care contributes to her being four times more likely to suffer anxiety than a man is. *The Female Brain*, 132.

10. Psychologist Simon Baron-Cohen, in *The Essential Difference: Male and Female Brains and the Truth About Autism* (New York: Basic Books, 2003), suggested that "the male brain is predominantly hard-wired for understanding and building systems." Vitz commented in turn that Baron-Cohen provided much evidence "that men are better at systematic, abstract, and problem-solving tasks. Males are more interested in mechanical objects, which are, of course, systems." *Complementarity*, 203. As for memory, Vitz noted that although women may have the advantage in "episodic" memory, men "have a better *semantic* memory — that is, for usually public (as opposed to

personal) facts, and abstract ideas." *Complementarity*, 201. See also Bruce Goldman, "Two Minds: The Cognitive Differences Between Men and Women," *Stanford Medicine*, Spring 2017, https://stanmed. stanford.edu/2017spring/how-mens-and-womens-brains-are-different.html.

11. Greg Bottaro, "On the Masculine Genius," *Humanum Review*, 2018, Issue 2.

12. Stein, *Essays on Women*, 95.

13. Vitz notes that, for men, "their status and accomplishments are much more central to their sense of well-being," and cites T. Kwang et al. "Men Seek Social Standing, Women Seek Companionship: Sex Differences in Deriving Self-Worth from Relationships," *Psychological Science* 24, no. 7 (2013): 1142–50, in *Complementarity*, 197.

14. John Paul II, Homily, Perth, Australia, November 30, 1986.

CHAPTER 5

1. John Paul II, *Man and Woman*, 90:2

2. Stein, *Essays on Women*, 72, 95.

3. John Paul II, *Mulieres Dignitatem*, 31.

4. Alice von Hildebrand, *The Privilege of Being a Woman* (Ypsilanti: Ave Maria University Communications, 2002), 36–37.

5. Ibid., 44.

6. Karol Wojtyla, *Love and Responsibility*, trans. H. T. Willetts (San Francisco: Ignatius, 1993 edition), 110–112.

7. Ibid., 113.

8. Ibid., 105.

9. Carl Anderson and Jose Granados, *Called to Love: Approaching John Paul II's Theology of the Body* (New York: Doubleday, 2009), 119.

CHAPTER 6

1. Yves R. Simon, *A General Theory of Authority* (Notre Dame, IN: University of Notre Dame Press, 1962), 64–65.

2. John Paul II, *Familiaris Consortio*, November 22, 1981, 25.

3. *Catechism of the Council of Trent for Parish Priests*, trans. John A. McHugh, OP, and Charles J. Callan, OP (New York: Wagner, 1923), 216.

4. Stein, *Essays on Women*, 77.

5. John Paul II, *Familiaris Consortio*, par. 25.

6. Pius XI, *Casti Connubii*, par. 27.

7. Ibid., par. 26.

8. Ibid., par. 28.

9. Bottaro, "On the Masculine Genius."

10. Stein, *Essays on Women*, 46.

11. Jane Austen, *Pride and Prejudice* (1813), Ignatius Critical Editions (San Francisco: Ignatius, 2008), 229.

12. Thomas Aquinas, *Commentary on the Gospel of Matthew*, tr. Jeremy Holmes and Beth Mortensen, ed. by the Aquinas Institute in 2 volumes (Lander, WY: The Aquinas Institute, 2013), e-text, aquinas.cc., #117.

13. John Paul II, *Redemptoris Custos*, August 15, 1989, par. 20.

14. Ibid.

CHAPTER 7

1. John Paul II, *Man and Woman*, 92:6.

2. Stein, *Essays on Women*, 132. She describes the feminine soul as "a shelter in which other souls may unfold."

3. Gary D. Chapman, *The Five Love Languages: How to Express Heartfelt Commitment to Your Mate* (Chicago: Northfield Publishing, 1995).

4. Von Hildebrand, *Privilege*, 56.

5. St. John Chrysostom, *On Marriage and Family Life*, trans. Catharine P. Roth and David Anderson (New York: St. Vladimir's Seminary Press, 1997), 54.

6. Pius XI, *Casti Connubii*, 27.

CHAPTER 9

1. John Paul II, *Man and Woman*, 89:3; cf. *Mulieres*, par. 24.

2. Ibid., 89:1–2.

3. John Paul II affirmed the asymmetry when he wrote, "Although the spouses should be 'subject to one another in the fear of Christ,' nevertheless in what follows, *the husband* is above all *the one who loves* and the wife, by contrast, is *the one who is loved*" (*Man and Woman*, 92:6). Though he does not emphasize "headship" and "submission" to the degree of his predecessors, John Paul II lays the foundation for the spousal relationship to be understood as an asymmetrical "gift dynamic" which, rather than contradict, serves to support a proper understanding of the Church's earlier authoritative teachings.

4. Pius XII, *Quando Alcuni*, Allocution on the Authority of Husband over Wife, September 10, 1941.

5. Kenneth Schmitz, *The Gift: Creation* (Milwaukee: Marquette University Press, 1982), 58–59.

6. Damian P. Fedoryka, "The Dignity of Man and the Dignity of Knowledge," *Faith and Reason,* vol. XIII, no. 1 (1987):4.

7. Frank Sheed, *Theology for Beginners* (New York: Angelico, 2011; originally by Sheed and Ward,

1957), 67, 164.

8. Federico Suarez, *Mary of Nazareth* (Princeton: Scepter, 1986), 235.

9. Alphonsus De Liguori, *The Glories of Mary* (New York: Kenedy & Sons, 1888), 468.

10. Suarez, *Mary of Nazareth*, 237.

11. Sheed, *Theology*, 67.

12. Catholic psychologist and author G. C. Dilsaver supports this idea as an "orthodox" interpretation of John Paul II's use of the term "mutual submission of the spouses." Such must "be seen as an analogous submission, where the man paradoxically submits himself to a life of authority that entails both headship and sacrificial service." (From "Karol Wojtyla and the Patriarchal Hierarchy of the Family," *Christian Order*, June/July 2002, http://christianorder.com/features/feature_2002-06-07_c.html)

13. Saint Augustine, *Sermo* 169, 11, 13.

14. *The Portable Dante*, trans. and ed. by Mark Musa (Penguin: New York, 1995), *Paradiso*, Canto III, 79–81.

ABOUT THE AUTHOR

MARY STANFORD studied philosophy at the University of Dallas and received a master of theological studies degree from the Pontifical John Paul II Institute for Studies on Marriage and Family in Washington, DC. A mother of seven, Mary is passionate about teaching. When she is not homeschooling her own children, she teaches a variety of courses in the Theology Department of Christendom College. Mary has spoken in dioceses across the country on topics including marriage, contraception, sexual complementarity, and the theology of the body. She has been married to her beloved Trey, an English professor, for twenty-two years.

YOU MIGHT ALSO LIKE

How to Be Miserable and Alone (Or Discover a Life That Truly Matters)
Kaiser Johnson

Kaiser Johnson, actor, athlete, and author, spent years listening to the lies of our culture, and through that this experience he has clearly identified 12 simple tricks to end up miserable and alone. He's tried all of them, and they work! It turns out hookup culture, self-fulfillment, self-love, using and abusing friends and family, maintaining a frantically busy schedule, and always taking the easy way out are the perfect recipe for a wretched life.

OSVCatholicBookstore.com or wherever books are sold.